THE
HARDMEN

ALSO BY THE VELOMINATI

The Rules

THE HARDMEN

LEGENDS AND LESSONS FROM THE CYCLING GODS

THE VELOMINATI

PEGASUS BOOKS
NEW YORK LONDON

The Hardmen

Pegasus Books Ltd
148 West 37th Street, 13th Floor
New York, NY 10018

First Pegasus Books hardcover edition November 2017

ISBN: 978-1-68177-570-8

10 9 8 7 6 5 4 3 2 1

Printed in the United States of America
Distributed by W. W. Norton & Company, Inc.

CONTENTS

FOREWORD

It's weird, you were so soft when you started, I remember thinking that. I thought you gave up too easy. Yet for some reason you've become harder than almost all of us, that's not normally what happens.

Christian Vande Velde to me, sometime in 2011

He was right of course, I didn't come into cycling to repeatedly bang my head against the proverbial wall, I came to win bike races in the same way my heroes Miguel Indurain and Maurizio Fondriest did. I didn't plan on all the hurting that would come with the 1,100 times I didn't win, not even mentioning the stuff that damaged me off the bike. I might have rethought it all if I had. Probably not, though. I still love it, you see, even with all the damage. And in truth I was like a moth to a flame when I discovered professional road racing; my fate was sealed there and then. It seemed so completely and utterly bonkers. I had no idea just how bonkers until I joined their ranks.

The rules were everywhere. The whole sport was dictated by them, they existed in the ethereal; well, they had to be since nobody ever bloody wrote them down. Each one of us had to learn them through the school of hard knocks; if you didn't learn, you didn't last. Yet, if you did, you graduated beyond the *neo-pro* stigma and became *un homme du métier* – which might translate into English as 'skilled in the art'.

I was a pretty good artist. That was even how the French would refer to me; *'L'Artiste'* (well, Cyrille Guimard would, though not in a positive way – more like a gentle put-down). To be fair, it was better than being *Le Dandy*, which they also called me. That was probably the time in my life Christian VdV was referring to when he said I was soft. He was right; a grain of sand could stop my machine (I actually read a *directeur sportif* say that about me in *L'Equipe*, which, by the way, didn't help our relationship).

The point of this is that I ended up cracking because of that softness, and making mistakes; doping, cheating, lying. All because of softness and a wrong love. I didn't stand up for my own values; I went too deep into a dark part of the *métier,* one that had always existed and was never really talked about; the one of doping. I went deep. I lost everything. Then I came back and fell in love with the sport all over again. I didn't care about their rules anymore, I only adhered to mine. In the process I became a harder and much better bike racer and, dare I say, person.

That's the point of this book; it's about the bike racers who made up their own rules. Because, as much as each of us must learn the rules from others at the beginning, it is only when we make them our own that we become hard.

David Millar

PROLOGUE

The trick, William Potter, is not minding that it hurts.

T. E. Lawrence, in *Lawrence of Arabia*

It is said that after his non-stop run from Marathon to Athens, Pheidippides immediately collapsed and died. Perhaps the most comprehensive example of athletic suffering imaginable; it also demonstrates the only sensible thing to do after running such a distance. This is the only mention we will make of running in this text. We are Cyclists, not savages.

The Velominati are dedicated to maintaining the cannon of Cycling's culture and etiquette in the form of The Rules. Cycling is a sport with a rich and colourful history; its traditions and codes of conduct have evolved over more than a century. The Rules (listed in full on p. 207) cover all aspects of this, ranging from states of mind (Rule #9 // If you are out training in bad weather, it means you are a badass. Period) to traditions (Rule #13 // If you draw race number 13, turn it upside down). And from aesthetics (Rule #14 // Shorts should be black, and Rule #33 // Shave your guns) to etiquette (Rule #43 // Don't be a jackass, but if you absolutely must be a jackass, be a funny jackass).

Chief among them is Rule #5:

Rule #5 // Harden the Fuck Up.

Rule #5, also known as The Five, or The V, is the essence of what it means to be a Cyclist: to persist in the face of intense suffering. It is a state of mind, bordering on a lifestyle. It means you are tough and disciplined, never following the path of least resistance. It *doesn't* mean you can't also fuss about with aesthetics or complain about the weather. But after you've finished faffing about with aesthetics and ancillary details you still submit to the deluge and go out and do your training.

Strength and pain are both transient things; they wax and wane not just with the rhythm of our training but with the cycle of our morale. Certainly the hours we pour into our sport play a crucial role in our fitness, but our minds play perhaps the biggest part. The mind is what dissociates pain and effort from the task at hand; it is the mind that silences the pleas coming from the body to yield. This is the essence of The Five.

Nearly every religion pays close heed to the concept – and the value – of suffering. The Buddhist approach is particularly helpful in its emphasis on experiencing things without clinging to them. Everything changes; embrace change and the fluidity of life. There is a beautiful freedom when you dissociate from the suffering; there is liberty in the realisation that how you endure suffering is a choice. This element of choice, what psychologists refer to as the Locus of Control, is part of what allows Cyclists to feel pleasure through suffering. (Either that or it's a personality disorder.) If we are to believe the white-bearded master computer program in *The Matrix*,[1] having a choice – even an illusory one – unlocks our sense of control and opens up an avenue of personal discovery by which we might learn something fundamental about ourselves or achieve some kind of salvation. Like Michelangelo wielding his hammer to chip away fragments of stone that obscure a great sculpture, we turn our pedals to chip away at our form, eventually revealing our true selves as a manifestation of hard work, determination and dedication.

---

1 Science-fiction film starring the dubious Keanu Reeves, in which computers take over the world and enslave the human population, while keeping them asleep and letting them think they are living out their lives in 1999. Which, contrary to the Prince song, was not one giant party.

As Cyclists, we choose to suffer; suffering liberates us from our daily lives. It presents itself in many forms: the pain of a climb, the cold of a rainy winter training ride, the unbridled fury at a clicking bottom bracket or insubordinate drivetrain. Life is a complicated mess of interdependencies in which we are more likely to be passengers than drivers; politicians, corporations, friends, family, morals, laws and physics routinely get in the way of us achieving our dreams. To ride our bikes and suffer by our own choice is to take control, if only for a short while, and escape into a more simple world.

But it goes beyond a state of mind and control over our uncontrollable lives. Suffering is also about taking care of ourselves mentally so we may each be a more complete person.

One evening, an elderly Cherokee brave told his grandson about a battle that goes on inside people.

He said, 'My boy, the battle is between the two wolves inside us all. One is evil. It is anger, envy, jealousy, sorrow, regret, greed, arrogance, self-pity, guilt, resentment, inferiority, lies, false pride, superiority, and ego.

The other is good. It is joy, peace, love, hope, serenity, humility, kindness, benevolence, empathy, generosity, truth, compassion and faith.'

The boy thought about this for a minute, then asked his grandfather, 'Which wolf wins?'

The old Cherokee simply replied, 'The one that you feed.'

Cherokee legend

We already ride for many reasons: the sense of freedom, the harmony, the feeling of flight as we hang, suspended, just a metre or so above the ground. There is the feeling of strength in our muscles as we force the tempo and near our threshold.

The demands of our lives mean that we can't always ride as much as we want or need to, and when we don't ride, our mental states start to deteriorate. Under these circumstances there is an enormous therapeutic value to climbing on a bike and going into the red, if only to remind ourselves that we can make ourselves hurt simply because we want to. We restore our confidence that we can do whatever needs to be done in life.

Other times an unexplained and unsolicited foul mood occurs, and it needs an exorcism. The best therapy in these situations is to make an appointment with The Man with the Hammer.[2] Just going for a ride doesn't flush the system; we need to run the motor on fumes for a bit in order to force a reboot. The policy is to keep turning on to a road that leads farther from home until the lights go out; only then are we permitted to ride home.

That ride through total exhaustion is where the magic happens; the sensation of hopelessness at the daunting road ahead slowly melts into certainty that we can override the messages coming from the body and keep tapping away at the task at hand. Eventually a heavy kind of dull strength returns to our muscles as the body finally decides to collaborate in the mission our Will has set it. By the time we get home, drained, we are reborn. We don't always need to ride in order to be a complete person, but generally we are better people when we find the time to turn the legs around and feed the Good Wolf.

Bicycle racing was born of a simple idea: to test the limits of human endurance. The first official race was held on 31 May 1868 at the Parc de Saint-Cloud in Paris, along a 1.2 kilometre course. Racing distances quickly grew: first to 20 km, then 50, 100, 200.

---

2 He stalks all Cyclists. He cannot be outridden or avoided. Everyone meets him eventually, and everyone remembers him. Ride long enough and hard enough and there he will be: hammer cocked – boom! – out go the lights. You are now riding in slow motion, children are running easily alongside, laughing and mocking. Congratulations, you have just met The Man with the Hammer.

In single-day events the ultimate test of endurance was reached with the 1,200 km Paris–Brest–Paris, which continues to this day as an amateur *randonnée* event, for which entry is restricted to people who have absolutely no appreciation for how far 1,200 km actually is.[3]

The first Tour de France, held in 1903, featured a route of 2,428 km in six stages: an average of 405 km per stage. By comparison, the twenty-one stages of the 2015 Tour's 3,360 km averaged only 160 km each. The bicycles in 1903 were leaden beasts with two gears on a flip-flop hub, meaning: get to the base of a climb, get off, loosen the wheel, turn it around, fix it in the 'low' gear. Get to the top, reverse the process. More cumbersome than the modern drivetrain, certainly, but the idea is still the same: go as fast as you can at the start, and as fast as you can at the finish. As for the middle: go as fast as you can.

They say a Cyclist is measured not by skill in riding a bicycle, but by their ability to suffer. The ones we revere the most are the ones who endure suffering especially well. We refer to them as the Hardmen. The Hardmen are the riders who relish a good fight and never give up. Quite simply, they are willing to venture deeper into the Pain Cave than anyone else is.

Not all Hardmen are the same. In this book we group them by the five traditional classifications of rider: *rouleurs*, *grimpeurs*, *klassiekers*, *domestiques* and *velocisti*. *Rouleurs* are all-rounders, possessed of a smooth, powerful style on the bike. They generate enormous speed for absurdly long periods of time, can climb well enough to be dangerous on the shorter ascents and go downhill as if they have no imagination whatsoever.

The *grimpeurs* are climbing specialists. Possibly the most

---

3 *Randonnées* are events in which Cyclists are generally expected to be responsible for their own care and feeding, in the original style and spirit of early bicycle racing.

mysterious of the Hardmen, these are tiny, waif-like riders who prosper due to a startling power:weight ratio and an enormous capacity for intense suffering in the high mountains, where gravity and thin air join forces to make the pain unbearable for mortals.

Klassiekers specialise in the one-day classic races held during the spring and autumn and often have a particularly unhinged penchant for the Cobbled Classics of early spring. These are big, tough riders who can produce the sort of sustained power that carries them at high speed over the brutal stone roads of northern France and Belgium, to emerge from the other side looking like grinning bog monsters.

The *domestiques* are team workers who labour in the wind day in and day out, in the service of their team leader. They perform all manner of thankless chores, from distributing food and drink from the team car, to setting the pace at the front of the bunch, to loaning out their bicycle or wheel if their leader has a mechanical problem.

Finally, the *velocisti* are the quick-fuse, short-twitch, fast riders in the bunch: the sprinters. They can bump shoulders and touch wheels at 60 kph, then unleash a ferocious turn of speed as the finish line approaches. This is a rare capacity, and makes for a particularly specialised type of rider: should the road point uphill, you will find these creatures wallowing at the back, cursing a blue streak at all the skinny little bastards who are leaving them in their dust.

All five types of rider can be judged by their results, certainly, but also – our favoured method – by their panache, heroism and humanity. The truly iconic riders became so through stories of their deeds.

The Keepers fell in love with Cycling during the '70s, '80s, '90s and beyond, and have become ever more obsessed with its history and legends.[4] Thus, our frame of reference leans towards

---

4 The Keepers of the Cog; the five principal authors of *Velominati*.

the riders who inspired us during that time and the myths about them that we discovered as we dug ever deeper into the sport. Also, we're more interested in riding our bikes than we are in doing things like 'research', so this book is written in true Velominati style: (ir)reverently and subjectively. We imagine that if it feels true, it probably is true. And if it happens to be wrong, then maybe being wrong makes it right.

When we convened our Hardmen Selection Jury, we quickly came to the realisation that we had many more subjects than we had room for, and we knew we couldn't spend the rest of our lives sitting in the Velominati bunker arguing, pint in hand, about which riders should be included. So we went with our favourite stories. And we certainly didn't worry about who was or wasn't allegedly doping.

These are the riders and rides that inspired us, and we hope they inspire you. We are the Velominati, and these are the Hardmen.

A NOTE ON STYLE

To reflect our reverence for Cycling heritage, we have chosen to name the five principal parts of this book in the language of the European peloton, which is to say usually French but occasionally Dutch or Italian, depending on which country is most fanatical about the type of rider in question. Hence *rouleur, domestique* and *grimpeur* are French, *klassieker* is Dutch (Flemish) and *velocista* Italian. Using the language of the peloton might come across as Europhile snobbery, but our intention is to express our respect for the culture of our sport. And possibly be a bit snobbish.

We also maintain a stylistic orthographical irregularity, capitalising the first letter of certain words in order to emphasise their significance within our vernacular. This includes Cycling, Monument, Pro and (of course) Hardman and any other word referring to something or someone we are quite certain has earned it.

Finally, we would like to emphasise that while we have endeavoured never to stray too far from the truth, we also hate to let facts get in the way of a good story. Witnesses, after all, nearly always destroy a fantastic tale.

PART I
LES ROULEURS

The frame lies forgotten in a dark corner of the workshop; it has been perhaps twenty years since it was last ridden. Hand-built of lugged steel tubing, it is a thing of beauty. Crafted by an artisan, it probably represented little more than a tool to its owner: a tool for inflicting suffering on himself and on those who dared follow his wheel. The paintwork tells a tale of countless hours of work by man and machine, their bond forged through their suffering. The paint on the top tube is pocked where it has absorbed the sweat that used to pour from the rider.

The owner of this frame could spend all day churning immense power through the pedals – on the front of the bunch or attacking, solo, with nothing but his shadow and the wind for company. This frame belonged to a *rouleur*. A *rouleur* is an all-rounder who rides well on most types of terrain. Rarely the best at any one discipline, but annoyingly strong, irrespective of the *parcours*.[1] Their secret power is the ability to dish out massive amounts of what we call The V for an unbearable length of time.[2] Usually wearing an expression of maniacal satisfaction.

Rouleurs and *domestiques* occupy some of the same space in Cycling: they can bring big power for hours on end and take pride in making others suffer.[3] The difference is that a *domestique* lacks the killer instinct of a *rouleur*. A *rouleur* is not only a strong rider but also a leader and a winner. *Rouleurs* lead from the front, they lead by

---

1 Not the relatively new sport wherein people jump around an urban landscape like uncaged monkeys but instead a classic Cycling term referring to the profile of a race route. Why don't we just say 'profile'? Because *'parcours'* is French and it is customary to adopt the old European terms for such things whenever possible in order to further mystify our sport to those not familiar with it. Compare use of *'terroir'* in wine-speak.

2 Shorthand for the Velominati's all-important Rule #5: 'Harden the Fuck Up'. The power of The V, or The Five, surrounds us, penetrates us and holds us together. Not unlike The Force, in fact, though it won't help you aim your photon torpedoes.

3 *Domestiques* are teammates who ride in service of their leader and thus rarely win races themselves. See Part IV.

Joop Zoetemelk (l) concedes the race to Eddy Merckx
(r) pre-start on account of his schoolboy loafers.

example; they suffer with the rest of their team, and when the team is done, they go out for another helping of pain.

Eddy Merckx, The Prophet, the greatest Cyclist of all time (and Elvis's *doppelgänger*), was the consummate *rouleur*. Team training sessions would always set out from his home in Brussels, departing *en masse,* to submit to the work that was required. Merckx would lead the rides, choosing the route on a whim, forcing the pace as he pleased. If anyone was dropped, it was their duty to find their own way home and, before the assembled team, explain precisely why they had humiliated themselves thus. That'll learn you.

A *rouleur* also generally exhibits the sporting quality we refer to as being the Perfect Amount of Dumb. That is to say, they are smart enough to do what is required to find peak fitness, disciplined enough to train in all kinds of weather and can manage a race tactically while hypoxic from effort. Yet they never question the wisdom of suffering so much for something so transient as riding their bicycle; they are just dumb enough that making it stop never occurs to them.

Rouleurs are some of the hardest of the hard riders. They are defined less by their size than by their style on the machine; a Magnificent Stroke tuned to sustained power, not to high revolutions or bursts of acceleration.[4] *Rouleurs* tend to be good time trialists and do well on short climbs, but when the race profile starts to look like the cardiogram of a teenage boy who just saw his first pair of boobs, they are usually to be found in the laughing group.[v]

Due to their wide power band, *rouleurs* are the riders who tend to study the race map, looking for the right terrain with the right kind of lumps if they're going to have a chance of being at the front. They are also possibly the most exciting to watch race; races of attrition suit them, as does bad weather – and when they're in the break, they're usually just dumb enough to take their strength for granted and overestimate themselves. Betting on the *rouleur* might be a gamble, but their style of racing often means that, even when they lose, it was a great show.

---

4 A rider's smooth, powerful stroke. *Pedal* stroke.
v Also known as the *gruppetto*: a group of riders joined together in bleak solidarity at the back of the race.

EDDY MERCKX, PART I

The Improbable Hour

The Hour Record is distinct from other Cycling events by being raced over a defined time, rather than distance. In a normal bicycle race the objective is to cover the prescribed route in the least possible amount of time. There is a not inconsiderable psychological benefit to this, and in fact it can drive us to push harder, especially when climbing. Upon sight of the crest of the hill we can tick down the gears and push harder just to make the suffering stop that much sooner.

The Hour Record is immune to such tactics. Suffer as much as you can, for an hour. No more, no less. Sixty minutes. And then count the laps to see how far you went. And that's not even the best part. We're not talking here about an undulating course where you gain speed on a descent, to carry over the next rise and ease the strain in the legs even if for a brief moment. We are talking about an hour on a velodrome's uncompromising track. The black line on the track represents a virtually flat oval along which the distance of the lap is measured. The rider must adhere as closely as possible to this line or sacrifice unmeasured distance; round and round for an hour, with a lap typically consumed in less than thirty seconds – quite a lot less if you are harbouring any hopes of breaking the record. Based on the size of

And so it was writ: none shall look better
suffering than The Prophet.

the velodrome and your target distance, challenging the record means around 120 laps or more, anticlockwise; hopefully you are better at turning left than Derek Zoolander.

Before their hour attempt, the rider will have determined how far they think they are capable of going, and will have scienced the shit out of things like average lap split times and even a specific lap-by-lap schedule they want to keep to, in order to have even a hope of meeting their goal. The other painful element here is that the rider is on a *track* bike, not a typical road bike; the gear is fixed, so there is no changing to an easier one when you realise you're fucked. The choice is final, and you won't know how good or bad your choice was until you are committed, much like that time your cousin double-dog-dared you to jump the water pipe on your skateboard.

For a hundie-odd laps, fighting dizziness and boredom are the least of your worries. Your biggest worries centre on the fact that, with every turn of the pedals, you are breaking down the fibres of your muscles one by one, leaving less functional muscle mass available for the next revolution of the pedals. Assuming one hundred revolutions per minute mostly because it makes the arithmetic simple and everyone hates complicated arithmetic, that's 60,000 revolutions of the pedals where your muscles are physically less capable of sustaining the required power than they could the revolution before. But still you have to maintain and sustain the effort; pacing is crucial.

There is a horrible joke about a young and old steer standing on a hilltop, looking down on a bunch of cows grazing in the valley below. The young steer says to the old, 'Let's run down there and fuck one of those cows!' The old steer says, 'What say we *walk* down there and fuck *all* of 'em.' The Hour is all about being the old steer.

Eddy Merckx was the Greatest Cyclist of All Time. Full Stop. Before Merckx set fixed wheel to track, the Hour Record had been broken twenty-three times, and by the most prestigious names in the sport. Fausto Coppi and Jacques Anquetil both held it; each was regarded as the greatest *rouleur* of his generation. But the man who first held and popularised the Hour Record was Henri Desgrange, who went on to found and organise the Tour de France. Henri was obsessed with figuring out ways to make Cyclists suffer more, to find better ways to make riding bicycles a test of human capability. And a long string of Cyclists submitted to this test, in search of an unbeatable Hour Record. At the time of Eddy's 1972 attempt that record had been set by the Dane Ole Ritter in 1968, with a distance of 48.653 km.

Setting an Hour Record necessitates going out with guns blazing but also being as consistent as possible in your lap times, due to the aforementioned malicious muscle-fibre-breakdown effect. Eddy, however, had other plans. There are minor records for the fastest 10 and 20 km efforts, which are unrelated to The Hour, but which he felt compelled to take on along the way, due to his insatiable appetite for winning things. This meant starting his effort like the young steer, but finishing like the old.

Merckx utilised every aerodynamic advantage available to him, including a special silk one-piece skinsuit and a custom frame built by Ernesto Colnago. He had his drivetrain and handlebars drilled out to remove all unnecessary material in an effort to make the bike as light as possible. His handlebar stem was the first ever made of titanium, a material poorly understood at the time; inspection of the stem reveals it was cut from a solid billet of metal and filed by hand to give the shape of a traditional stem. The file marks remain visible.

Merckx, of course, set a new Hour Record of 49.43 km, but the effort meant he had to be carried from his bicycle. After he had composed himself, he said:

> Throughout this hour, the longest of my career, I never knew a moment of weakness, but the effort needed was never easy. It's not possible to compare the Hour with a time trial on the road. Here it's not possible to ease up, to change gears or the rhythm. The Hour Record demands a total effort, permanent and intense, one that's not possible to compare to any other. I will never try it again.

He later said the effort took a year off his career; I'm only glad it was from the tail end and not the front end or middle bit.

A full eight years later it took one Francesco Moser with an ultra-high-tech aerodynamic bike to break Merckx's record. Moser's record stood until the 1990s, when Chris Boardman and Graeme Obree traded the record, using ever-evolving time trial positions. The technology was advancing more quickly than the UCI (Union Cycliste Internationale) had a stomach for, so it issued new regulations that prohibited all but the most basic bicycle design.[1] Going a step further (back), in 1997 they modified the Hour regulations to stipulate that all future attempts be made on a 'Merckx-style' bicycle: round tubes, spoked wheels and drop handlebars. All prior records set using aerodynamic equipment were reclassified as 'Best Human Effort' distances, and Merckx's 49.43 km mark was re-established as the official Hour Record.

The first rider to attempt this new (old) Merckx-style record was Chris Boardman, who broke it by a whopping 10 metres. Boardman was the consummate bicycle geek, going so far as to work with Royce, a small component manufacturer based in England, not only to build him a near-frictionless set of hubs and bottom bracket but also to develop special spoke nipples that were recessed into the rims. Boardman was delighted with this innovation and convinced of the aerodynamic gain it would bring. (Years later he took the bike to a wind tunnel where, ironically, it was determined that his aero nipples provided virtually no measurable advantage, apart from the obvious mental one.)

In 2015 the UCI finally came to its senses and updated the regulations to allow the kind of aero machinery universally used in time trials; this set off a flurry of attempts which culminated with Bradley Wiggins's monster distance of 54.5 km at the Lea Valley velodrome, track-cycling home of the London Olympics in 2012.[2]

---

1 The Union Cycliste Internationale is Cycling's governing body. Sometimes referred to as the *Union Cycliste Irrationale*, it's the sort of bureaucratic organisation that hinders more than it governs. It turned a blind eye to the rampant doping that took place in Cycling during the 1990s and 2000s but felt compelled to limit the innovation that was taking place in bicycle technology.
2 It is worth remembering that Chris Boardman's Best Human Effort was nearly 56.4 km in 1996, so Wiggo still technically got punked.

NICOLE COOKE

Birth of a Hardwoman

No Cyclist avoids suffering, but some seek to limit it while others choose to embrace it. And then we have a handful of characters who consider playing Whack-a-Mole with The Man with the Hammer to be good sport, particularly when playing the part of Mole.

In the current climate it's impossible not to consider the impact that doping has on our sport. Most of us have watched professional bike racing and delighted in the spectacle throughout the years, aware to varying degrees that doping is part and parcel of the sport we love so much. In the past score of years or so we've gone so far as to assume that most – if not all – riders are doping: a regrettable situation but one that has done little to temper our enthusiasm as fans. After all, when all the riders are doing it, then surely what we're watching is a level playing field of willing participants who understand how the game is played. Cheaters cheating cheaters almost feels like fair play.

It's all beautifully convenient so long as all the riders are doping (and so long as you don't understand too much about how doping actually works). This is not the case, however; there *are* those who have raced, and are racing, clean, against dopers. These riders are truly being cheated out of a career by a

Jazz hands!

culture that not only turns a blind eye to cheating, but that also ostracises those who don't. There are only a few riders in the last several generations who have made a strong vocal and plausible case that they competed without the use of performance-enhancing drugs or methods of any kind. Edwig Van Hooydonk was one, Nicole Cooke was another.

Nicole has been a force in women's Cycling since turning Pro in 2002. A powerful *rouleur*, she excelled on every terrain and in any race format, and was nigh-on unbeatable in uphill finishes, taking a total of three La Flèche Wallonne Féminine titles, each of which required such a laying down of The V that it brought her to collapse. Cooke raced at the top of her sport for thirteen years; she scaled the heights of achievement with wins in every major race on the calendar, including the Ronde van Vlaanderen voor Vrouwen, La Flèche, the Giro d'Italia Femminile, the Grande

Boucle Féminine Internationale,[1] the Olympic Road Race and the World Championship Road Race. What's more, she accomplished all of it while remaining staunchly anti-doping, to the point that she faced sackings for refusing doping products.

There is a tale of Cooke sharing a team house early on in her career. She popped to the refrigerator for a slice of cake or whatever, and behind some cartons of milk she spotted various bottles and vials and syringes. She must have wondered for a moment whether she had accidentally opened Riccardo Riccò's fridge instead of her own.[2] She phoned her mentor and mindfulness coach (her dad) and talked the situation over.

It must be astoundingly difficult to face such a scenario as a brand new Pro, having just left home to start your career. From the age of twelve Cooke had committed her life to Cycling. From there it was one step after the other in a methodical and unrelenting battle to ascend to the world stage. She raced hard and trained hard. She largely funded her own racing programme because British Cycling was grossly under-funding and under-supporting women's Cycling at the time. She left school and

---

1 The women's Tour de France – or one version of it, at any rate – held from 1984 until 2009. In its heyday it shared the final podium presentation with the men on the Champs-Élysées, but then it suffered organisational and funding challenges that led to its demise.
2 Riccardo Riccò was a Cyclist in the mid-2000s who raced on some of the dodgiest teams and produced some of the dodgiest results. He burst on to the scene as a neo-Pro and was immediately competing at the highest level, dropping the world's best climbers regularly. He was popped for doping during the 2008 Tour de France and served a two-year ban. Upon his return he famously attempted to administer a do-it-yourself blood transfusion which landed him in hospital and nearly killed him. Undeterred, he was later caught trying to buy EPO in a McDonald's parking lot. Unable to find a team willing to take him on, he now seeks fame pursuing 'King of the Mountain' titles on Strava, a social network for runners and Cyclists, for the world's most famous climbs. No doubt aboard a motorcycle.

went to Europe with everything stitched to a single dream: to become the dominant female Cyclist of her generation.

Barely weeks into her first stint abroad she faced her first test: the first temptation to dope. This is *le métier*, the work of the professional Cyclist; all the training and sacrifice that goes into preparing for competition, but in context it also includes the various doping practices that are (or were) required in order to be at one's best. It is a lesson most riders learn early. In the balance hang all the sacrifices they've ever made – the education, the training, the youth spent early to bed when friends are off to the pub – against the first step along a slippery slope. Many understandably choose to step along that slope.

But not Nicole. She knew that even condoning the presence of the products in the house – whatever they were – was to begin that journey of small concessions that irrevocably end in doping. She cleared the refrigerator out and chucked its contents in the bin outside the house. 'Either the gear goes, or I go.'

The gear went and Nicole stayed, knowing she could only start her journey if she was going to race clean. How many such trials would she face? No one but she will ever know, but one thing is for certain: she became the first British rider to win the Olympic Road Race. Then she became the first rider of any nationality to win the Olympics and the World Championships in the same year.

Cycling is hard. Racing is harder. Racing clean among dopers is even more harderer. Not just in physical terms, but also in its challenges to your ethics, your morals and your character.

SEAN YATES

Always full gas

Why do the Velominati admire Sean Yates so? Two of the Keepers of the Cog are big men – *rouleurs*, we'd like to think – so riders like Sean Yates suit us just fine. In our dreams we are not climbers like Carlos Sastre, crossing the mountaintop finish line with a dummy in our mouths. No, we are Yates-like: too big to climb, sitting on the front of the peloton, keeping a steady yet hellish pace through the rolling landscape, for hours. And no, we don't carry a fucking dummy in our jersey pocket to pull out just in case we do solo off the front to victory. Mrs Yates is back at home taking care of the damn baby, I've got a bloody job to do here, and that job is to ride hard enough and long enough and steady enough at the front, so no one is going to put their nose into the wind or get any wild ideas about attacking. And when we do descend off a climb, I'll be on the front again to lead you all down stupidly fast. Don't you touch them brakes, you ponces.

Too much climbing spells trouble for the *rouleur*. Yet if climbing *is* involved, the suffering on the way up can be paid back on the descent. The *rouleur* has the mass to drop like a stone, so is usually a more than handy descender. Our boy Sean Kelly, quite some descender in his day, relates an encounter with Yates: 'I'd been trying to ride into form for the Tour de France,' says Kelly, and when I lost contact with a group of Colombians on the climb I rode within myself. There was a break gone anyway so I wasn't threatening the stage or the GC [General Classification – ed.]. I was pretty good at descending [no shiet – ed.], so I left the group I was with as we started making the descent and was catching the next group as quickly as I dared. All of a sudden this thing came past me and I thought, 'Feck! What the hell was that?' I assumed it was a motorbike, but of course it was Yates. I remember there was a straight bit then a chicane, all of it awash with water, and I thought, 'Jaysus, he'll never make that.' He did, though.

Sean Yates takes up the story ...

He [Kelly] rode up to me the next day and said, 'What were you doing down there, you lunatic? There was no way you could have won the stage, the break was long gone.'

I just shrugged my shoulders. 'I like riding downhill, I suppose.'

Sean Yates, *It's All About the Bike*

As a proper *rouleur*, Sean gained most of his victories in time trials and even wore the *maillot jaune* in the Tour.[1] At the height of his powers he earned his pay cheque as a *gregario* for the American Motorola team.[2] In fact, it was Yates who schooled a

---

1 The *maillot jaune* is the yellow jersey worn by the race leader in the Tour de France. Wearing this for one day bestows a certain amount of honour for the rest of one's life.

2 The Velominati make a distinction between *gregario* and *domestique* (see p. 198). We generally believe the French language is the best at describing the Cycling world. Yet *domestique* suggests domestic servant, while *gregario* implies friend. At Motorola, Sean Yates was a part-time road captain (an experienced rider who can see how the race is unfolding and direct teammates from the peloton) with almost ten years as a Pro behind him, a point man when high tempo and major suffering were required ... and just a big badass. Doesn't every team with its fair share of wee climbers also need a big badass?

certain brash Texan in the ways of the European racing scene. When Sean Yates tells you what to do, you listen.

The photograph overleaf is of the young Yates suffering on the nearly 300 km (180 mile) route of Milan–Sanremo, 1983. This race, known as 'La Primavera', the first Monument of the season, may have come a bit early for Yates in '83.[3] His arms are the arms of a normal healthy adult, not the ineffective twigs of a Cyclist. And he is consequently suffering like an animal.[4]

Graham Watson tells of being on a moto as they rode past riders on the Capo Berta.[v] Watson was looking through his viewfinder when Yates came alongside. Yates's suffering made Watson *almost* feel bad for taking the picture. Almost. *Chapeau*, Graham Watson.[6] The deeper secret is that earlier that day Yates had given most of the food from his *musette* to the starving Watson and was now meeting a certain man with a certain hammer.[7]

The next picture is of Sean blasting through a corner in Paris–Roubaix.[8] Looking good while racing Paris–Roubaix is a

---

3 A Monument is like a golf Major (what is golf?) or a Grand Slam tournament in tennis (but way harder and with less grunting). Winning one of the big five Classic races – Milano–Sanremo, Ronde van Vlaanderen, Paris–Roubaix, Liège–Bastogne–Liège and Giro di Lombardia – ensures Legend status for the rider, even if that's all they ever win.
4 'Animal' became one of Yates's nicknames.
v A moto is a motorcycle carrying a gendarme, photographer, TV cameraperson or French ex-Pro *avec* microphone doing live commentary.
6 *Chapeau*: Literally, 'hat', which we figuratively doff to heroic riders and, on occasion, cold-hearted photographers.
7 A *musette* is the cotton throwaway lunch bag handed to riders during a race so they can eat on the bike. It is snatched at speed and looped over the head; contents are inspected for insertion into jersey pocket, immediate inhalation or immediate ejection. Many a rider has come to grief at the 'feed zone', where bidons fire sideways from the peloton like decoy flares from a military transport in a war zone.
8 Possibly the hardest single-day race of the year. It is one of the five

*The camera adds 10 pounds. Which
makes you look 40 pounds too fat.*

Hardman speciality, and it is not easy to look good riding across
manure-soaked cobbles. In evidence are the Yates signature
short shorts. Sean was partial to showing more gun than most.[9]

Monuments of racing. It takes place in northern France on the second
Sunday in April, and winning it requires equal amounts of great strength
and bike handling. Whole books have been written on just this race,
which is a race for Hardmen.

9 Cycling slang for legs. Also cannons, howitzers. The role of such
weaponry was described as the 'Last Argument of Kings' by Louis
XIV, who had the phrase engraved in Latin (*Ultima ratio regum*) on his
artillery pieces – a practice that the celebrated author Chris Cleave has
suggested the committed Cyclist might adopt with his or her big ring. It is
obligatory to compare one's quadriceps (not biceps – we are Cyclists, not,
as we may have mentioned already, savages) to military tools of death and
destruction. For example, 'Did you hear the guns of Navarone echoing
across the valley yesterday afternoon? That was me on the golf course hill.'

40 pounds lighter and 40 pounds radder.

He pulled them up like that so he didn't show his tan lines when wearing Bermuda shorts back at the house. Dodgy as fuck, but it was a Sean Yates trademark. Sean was always given free rein for Paris–Roubaix; as a *rouleur* and Hardman, he was a natural for this brutal race.

The last photo is of Sean Yates as *directeur sportif* for Team Sky.[10] Yes, he looks like the cop who shot Paul Newman in *Cool*

---

10 *Directeur sportif* is a French term for the guy who sits in the team car and tells his riders what to do. Unless that rider is Eddy Merckx. No one tells Eddy what to do.

What we've got here is failure to communicate ...
The only Pro to get thinner in retirement.

Hand Luke. And yes, he appears to be rail-thin, thinner even than when racing. No one is going to be dropping back to the team car to moan about 'not feeling good, down there' when Sean is driving. Once a Hardman, always a Hardman.

MARIANNE VOS

2012 Olympic Road Race

V – not for victor, but for Rule #5!

Northern Europeans are good at bad weather. It's an occupational hazard, living where it rains more than it suns. If you don't enjoy riding in the wet, you won't enjoy riding very much. The 2012 Women's Olympic Road Race brought to mind Peter van Petegem's advice at Paris–Roubaix in 2002, along the lines of 'This weather is good for us. It has already defeated most of the field.' (See p. 138 for the full story.)

The 2012 women's race was held in the sort of deluge where some spectators claimed they saw animals lining up in pairs along the roadside. Most of the riders would have inwardly capitulated when they first pulled back the curtains to see water flowing down from the heavens. Most, but not all. Marianne Vos makes one reconsider the definition of the term *rouleur*. She is an all-rounder of unprecedented versatility, having won virtually every event at the world élite professional level, on the dirt, on the track or on the road. (While she's never won a world championship on a mountain bike, she has won World Cup events and has a closet full of Dutch National Championship jerseys.)

She is a lithe, powerful rider with a similar physique to Lizzie Deignan (née Armitstead), another great *rouleur*. Both can win sprints on a flat *parcours* just as well as they can win a hilly road race solo or from a small group. The secret to both riders' versatility lies in a balanced set of riding abilities and exceptional mental strength; whatever the terrain or the race situation, they will find a way to win because they rarely wait for another rider to dictate tactics. They race from the front and write the script for the race before the competition does.

The 2012 Men's Olympic Road Race was set to be one of the most remarkable races of the year, or possibly decade. Mark Cavendish was to be the winner on home turf, with the full support of Team GB. The reality was very different, which is why we should all make a habit of avoiding reality. The route seemed perfect: just enough climbing to make it hard, but just enough flat and fast bits to open the race up. Truth be told, though, the men's race was a snoozer, with the dubious Alexander Vinokourov, fresh off a ban for blood-doping, taking the win after allegedly buying off his breakaway companion. What a contrast to the women's race.

Marianne, however many feathers she already had in her hat,

had yet to win the Olympic Road Race. In fact, winning world road championship titles had proved hard enough; she took the World Élite title at nineteen, but had then finished second almost every year since. So she had the proverbial monkey on her back, to say the least.

The break went early; too early. It resulted from an attack by none other than Mary V, who would rather lose a race than sit in the bunch waiting for others to decide the race for her. This move was bold even for her; perhaps it was the sopping wet roads and the risk of crashes in the bunch that spurred her to form a smaller, safer group. In road racing sometimes the early breakaway stays away because the group has the right composition of riders in it, meaning that none of the teams in the main group has a reason to chase down their own rider. This was the case here, and it kept all the big countries from chasing; the Netherlands had Mary V, Great Britain had Lizzie Deignan, the United States had Shelley Olds – who was sure to win in a group sprint – and Russia had Olga Zabelinskaya. For the bunch behind, it was a matter of controlling the race; for the group up the road, it was a matter of full gas though an onslaught of rain and pain for three and a half hours.

The big difference between a good bike race and a rubbish bike race sometimes comes down to this: a group of favourites working together rather than playing games, racing hard, in harmony, to stay ahead of the pack. And then, when the finish line comes into view, all bets are off. In recent years men's racing seems to have gained a formulaic feeling to it: on a flat *parcours* the breakaway will be caught close to the finish line; on hilly terrain, the winning move will come from one hard attack with only a few kilometres left to come. Robots on bikes controlled via the race radio sometimes seem to have replaced riders reading the race and attacking with panache. Women's racing, on the other hand, has been setting the bar high in this respect; the races are aggressive and unpredictable, and the riders act more on impulse and guts than on formula and instructions from the team car.

Shelley Olds flatted out of the lead group, which meant that approaching the finish were three women, each of them already in the medals and each of them within an even strike of taking home the gold. Olga drew the short straw and found herself at the front, leading out the other two as they lined up for the final sprint: Lizzie and Marianne, both good sprinters, both with an armchair ride to the line on the Russian Express. Vos wanted it most and didn't wait for Lizzie to make her move; she started the sprint early, spraying Lizzie with her rooster tail the entire way to the finish.[1]

Class is taking control of your fate, forcing the move and then asserting yourself when it counts. Leave it all on the road, or lose trying. This was a race won in the style of the great Eddy Merckx himself.

---

1 The rooster tail is the watery spray from the rear wheel of a bicycle in the rain. Far from being a refreshing spritz of rainwater, it is a gritty mess filled with whatever lies on the road: sand, manure and all manner of things best left to your imagination.

EDDY MERCKX, PART II

Belgium, April 1971

Liège–Bastogne–Liège was a race that didn't have a course that suited me, so I rarely rode it. One year I had a call the day before from team manager Franco Cribiori to say that Roger De Vlaeminck, the star of the Brooklyn team, was ill and wouldn't start. That meant I had to race, as I was the No. 2 in the team. I left Ghent on the Saturday afternoon with my father to drive down: a slow drive as there was no motorway. We were driving down the main road from Brussels to Liège, it was raining and snowing together, the worst possible conditions for riding a bike. A long way up ahead we spotted a cyclist on the road: we couldn't work out who would be riding in such weather. It was so bad there was no one else outside. When we passed the bike rider we saw it was Merckx: he was riding the hundred kilometres from Brussels to Liège, all alone, because he had not won Flèche Wallonne during the week. He won Liège–Bastogne–Liège the next day by five minutes ahead of the second rider: I climbed off after forty kilometres.

Patrick Sercu, quoted in William Fotheringham,
Merckx: Half Man, Half Bike

Distil the world of Cycling down to this story and declare victory. How would the conversation have gone between Patrick

Hey, weather. Go fuck yourself.

and his father, as they drove past? Maybe nothing, maybe just that Belgian 'phoof'. Words won't suffice.

The decision to ride to Liège the day before the race, in shit weather, was Eddy's and Eddy's alone. If anything, his *directeur sportif* would have tried to talk him out of it. No doubt his wife was the only one in on his plan; she would have driven down with the extra kit and a thermos of soup. Would this ever happen today? No. You can't pay riders to be like this. A *directeur sportif* wouldn't even make his team leader do this, even if he was really pissed off at his overpaid star. Being a Hardman comes from within. A Hardman knows that, in terrible conditions, he can outlast his foes even if he has bad legs on. At the top level of Cycling it is a mental battle as much as a physical one. Eddy was so dominant that his enemies often knew they were beaten at the start line. It was more a matter of how the beating would be handed out. Yet even this was not enough. Merckx was so disgusted by his Flèche Wallonne performance that a solid 100 km ride the day before Liège would be just the thing he needed.

Maybe that thought would also have occurred to Roger De Vlae-minck (the defending champion) had he not been ill, but when that day dawned sleety and wet, it was only Eddy who actually threw a leg over his bike and rode from the house.

The next day's race was a true Merckx victory. The weather was not unlike the day before. He attacked 92 km from the finish: a suicidal move even by his standards. And Eddy *did* fade as he neared the finish and was caught by a fellow Belgian, Georges Pintens. But Eddy was not to be denied in the final sprint. Merckx was so flattened by the effort in those conditions he had to shower sitting on a chair. Was his training ride the previous day more than just training? It gave him the confidence to know he could attack from a long way out, in terrible conditions, when all others would have had doubts.

Much will be made of not avoiding training if the weather is less than nice. The conditions are what they are, and we must train in them, always. Riding on a trainer in the garage is something, but it's not really hill-repeats in the rain, is it? This speaks to mental training too, like Eddy's ride to Liège – many will be beaten at the starting line in bad weather. Make bad weather your ally, not your enemy; the best way to do that is to get out there and train in it. It's only some wet and cold. Besides, as Sean Kelly says (see p. 103), you won't know how wet and cold it really is until you get back from the ride.

REBECCA TWIGG

Mind over Matter

You can accomplish so much with a strong will. Just do your best, no matter what. Don't let negative thoughts creep in. Don't talk yourself out of anything.

Rebecca Twigg

In 1969, on a road somewhere in Czechoslovakia, Audrey McElmury won the World Championship road race. It had been fifty-seven years since the Star-Spangled Banner had been played at a Cycling event, and the race organisers had to delay the podium presentations until someone could find a copy of the US national anthem. The 1970s saw US women collect seventeen World medals, with more than a third of them gold. In other words, while men's Cycling was being dominated by riders like Eddy Merckx and Bernard Hinault, with only a handful of Americans venturing on to the European racing scene, women's Cycling was being shaped by English-speaking riders, most of them Americans. (In fact, the first women's version of the Tour de France, held in 1984 – the now defunct Tour de France Féminin – was won by the American Marianne Martin.)

While the American women were lighting up the international

USA, 1st and 2nd: that will never happen again.

racing scene, Rebecca Twigg was lighting up the roads around Washington University in Seattle. Having skipped high school and jumped right into university at the tender age of fourteen, she was also busy drag-racing motor vehicles on her Huffy. Some time in 1977 it occurred to her to try her hand at racing, and she won state titles on the track as well as on the road. She then quickly graduated from state to national champion, again on both track and road.

She carried on road racing with great success – taking the silver medal in a photo finish against teammate Connie Carpenter in the 1984 Olympic road race. But it was on the track that her dominance was undisputed. She became a six-time World Pursuit Champion, inspiring legions of both male and female track racers in the US. Velominati community member @Haldy tells of racing Nationals in the 1990s, while just a budding Velominatus getting serious about turning left in a velodrome. Twigg was warming up for the pursuit on the rollers in a jersey, with her skinsuit tied around her waist. Rollers, for anyone who has ridden them, are a touch tricky to ride even on a road bike with gears. On a fixed-gear bike, let alone a pursuiting machine, it requires maximum skill. To ride them no-handed is asking to wind up in a heap on the floor.

@Haldy tells of watching in awe as Rebecca sat up to ride no-handed while she took off her jersey and pulled on the skinsuit. He vowed to learn to do the same and felt he arrived as a Master some twenty years later when he was warming up at Nationals himself and performed the same feat. (We wince at the thought of a Master going shirtless in a velodrome, the same as you do. For that image, we ask your forgiveness.)

Rebecca's breakthrough Hardwoman moment came at her first appearance at the World Track Championships. This was the '80s, and the '80s was all about the USSR. The USSR was so big back then (give or take a decade) that the Beatles wrote a song about it because they were afraid they might not be as big as the USSR. Having progressed through the heats of the individual pursuit, Twigg found herself paired up against the two-time defending World Champion Nadesja Kibardina in the quarter-final. A rookie 'Murcan against a veteran Rooskie – no points for guessing who's going to win that one. But Rebecca had a moment of clarity just prior to the start of her event: she acknowledged that she was in awe of her competitor, then suddenly realised that Kibardina was just an athlete, the same as her, there for the same reason she was: to compete and win bike races. A Rooskie might be hard to beat, but another athlete? Well, I beat those all the time, she thought, what's different about this one?

Nothing, as it turns out. She crushed Kibardina. And she won her semi-final as well. And then, when she paired up against her countrywoman Connie Carpenter for the final, she beat her too. Behind every legend is a real, live human. And every human can be beaten. It is the will that overcomes.

JACKY DURAND

Go Long or Go Home

Whomever said 'to look good is already to go fast' wasn't Jacky Durand. He went fast wearing that kit.

Do you ever think about legacy? About death, and how you'd like to be remembered? What would you like inscribed on your headstone? For this particular French Hardman,[1] a line from

---

1 Some may argue that this term is an oxymoron these days, but we refer you to one B. Hinault. Any arguments may be taken up with him.

his Wikipedia page would probably do nicely: 'Jacky Durand became celebrated for long, lone attacks, which sometimes succeeded but usually didn't.'

While most of our heroes will be remembered for their great wins, Durand will mainly be remembered for failing. But failing in the most spectacular and determined way possible, by going on long breakaways, either with some other masochists or, more often, on his own. Which suited him just fine. And when it paid off, it paid off big time. Two French National Championships, two combativity awards, a prologue victory and a few days in yellow at the Tour, a win Paris–Tours. Most Pros would be pretty happy with that *palmarès*.[2] Dudu's crowning glory, though, came at the Tour of Flanders, the Ronde van Vlaanderen, arguably the most prestigious Monument of them all.[3]

The word 'win' probably wasn't included in Jacky's race notes that cool, crisp morning in April 1992. His notes probably read more like: 'Get in early break, whittle them down, survive until swept up by main protagonists, roll in, have post-ride coffee.' Maybe he wouldn't have written 'protagonists'. Maybe 'big bastards'. After all, he would need all his energy for a day of hammering along off the front in the wind – which only ever seems to blow from the front – rather than wasting it on finding the right adjective to describe those he'd probably despise later on when they passed him and he tried his best to stifle his wails to the sweet baby Jesus.

---

2 Prize list. A fancy French term for your CV or resumé, essentially.
3 Dudu is the term of endearment given to Durand by the French. The French probably don't realise it sounds like a childish term for 'poop' in English, but that makes it feel a little bit like an inside joke, doesn't it? The Ronde van Vlaanderen, also known as the Ronde or the Tour of Flanders, is, along with Paris–Roubaix, arguably the hardest one-day race of the year. It's long: almost every climb is a cobbled, steep bottleneck. The positioning race to get to the foot of each *berg* is hellish. If you arrive at a climb halfway back in the peloton, your race is over.

When he worked his way into the break of a dozen or so riders, the big bastards would have had a chuckle to each other: 'Huh huh, there goes Dudu again.' Maybe a betting pool was started to see who could guess how far from the finish the pack would sweep him up. Some cruel swine would have had a few francs on a last-kilometre catch, just because bike riders are inherently cruel swine. Maybe Thomas Wegmüller had a bet each way as well, as he was the last man to stay with Jacky as they approached the finale, consisting of the decisive ascents of the Muur van Geraardsbergen (Kapelmuur) followed closely by the Bosberg. Neither would have expected to reach this point at the head of affairs, that's a sure bet. Durand had told his *directeur* that he was 'cooked' well before the brutal Muur was tackled, and it was only the work being done by the Swiss monster Wegmüller that allowed Durand to hang on as long as he did. He expected Wegmüller to attack on the Muur, but instead he found himself easily able to match the seemingly stronger rider. The tactic that would win him the race was one he'd witnessed Edwig Van Hooydonck use to great effect in his two Ronde wins, which was to attack hard on the Bosberg. From mere survival to the prospect of actually winning, the Bosberg turned it all around, and suddenly Durand was 20 seconds up and not looking ready to die just yet. Fatigue and adrenaline make a fierce cocktail.

Broken both physically and mentally, Wegmüller gave up the chase and Durand knew the race was his. And at this moment Jacky had a vision of God talking to him, praising him and anointing him as he drove alongside in an old Peugeot. That's probably not so far-fetched; the pain-addled brain sends out all kinds of weird messages. But when you're about to win a Monument and The Prophet (Eddy Merckx, *bien sûr*) himself pulls up next to you, then you're forgiven for thinking you're hallucinating. But this was real, Jacky Durand was about to win the Ronde and he was having a chat with Eddy Merckx:

All of a sudden the race director's car pulled up to me and Eddy
Merckx stuck out his head and said, 'Kid, you're going to win the
Tour of Flanders!' And I was like 'God has spoken!' I'd never met
Merckx, but I figured if he was telling me that I was going to win the
Tour of Flanders, well, he was probably right!

From that moment on, Durand would try the long-break tactic
virtually every time he raced. Turn on the telly for the Tour high-
lights show every night at six o'clock, and there'd be Jacky chug-
ging along, exactly where he wanted to be; alone at the front, and
on the TV. Fans would actually bet on how far from the line he'd
be caught. It is unlikely anyone ever wagered on him making
it in ahead of the pack, and that's exactly how this great escape
artist worked: everything hinged on luck, miscalculation from
the peloton, good legs and pure old-fashioned stoneground guts.

M. Durand was a true racer – a dying breed these days.

ANNIE LONDONDERRY

Anything You Can Do,
I Can Do Better

Riding a bike is, fundamentally, an incredible experience: the wind in your face, the sensation of generating speed under your own power, the balance of forces that almost magically hold the bike suspended upright. For most of us as children this mystical experience was coupled with a profound sense of liberation as our mobility expanded exponentially. Our radius of travel, previously limited by how far we could walk, grew by an order of magnitude. With this growth came our first sense of autonomy. We no longer needed to persuade our parents to take us where we wanted to go; we could decide to make the journey ourselves.

The bicycle meant freedom, and not just for children. The development of the bicycle during the late 1800s and early 1900s meant freedom for women at large, emerging as it did, just as the Women's Rights movement was gathering momentum. Suddenly women could take control of their own transport and achieve a measure of autonomy. With it came a challenge to the accepted codes of social etiquette and even clothing, as corsets and long skirts gave way to bloomers (named after Amelia Bloomer) and blouses.

*There was a rumour floating around that if you smile
on camera, you would look like a crazy person.*

Let me tell you what I think of bicycling. I think it has done more to
emancipate women than anything else in the world. It gives women
a feeling of freedom and self-reliance.

Susan B. Anthony

Big change polarises opinion; there will be those who embrace it and those who resist. Both groups tend to be vocal; one attempting to demonstrate their progressive thinking, the other attempting to demonstrate their appreciation for propriety.

The exact details are lost in the mists of time, but apparently individuals representing just such groups fell to bickering over the capabilities of women in an exclusive club somewhere in Boston. One claimed that a woman was capable of any feat a man was; the other disagreed. At the time society was set abuzz by the feat of Thomas Stevens, who had cycled around the world in fifteen months, raising $5,000 in the process. A wager was set between two men over whether a woman could match that feat.

Enter Annie, a mother of three who had never thrown leg over top tube in her life, but who accepted the challenge. She hopped on a fixed-gear bike with nothing but a change of clothes and a pistol, and set off into the sunset. Or into the damp Boston fog. Whichever it was, she set off into it and began a journey both physical and spiritual.

She quickly came to a few conclusions that might seem obvious to the modern Cyclist. First, fixed-gear bikes are great for the track (and for commuting, if you believe the hipsters). Second: skirts and corsets restrict both motion and breathing. Tired of lifting her feet off the pedals and praying for a safe delivery to the bottom of every hill along the eastern seaboard, she swapped her fixie for a Sterling, the state-of-the-art bicycle of the day. She also switched from skirts to bloomers before eventually changing into a men's riding suit. Whatever the fuck a 'riding suit' is. Sounds horrific.

She made her journey from Boston to New York, and then on to France.[1] From there she travelled by bike, train and steam-

---

1 Although we never like to let the facts get in the way of a good story, she actually started going west to Chicago before realising that winter in the American Midwest is a little more Rule #9 than anyone at the turn of

boat to Alexandria, Colombo, Singapore, Saigon, Hong Kong, Shanghai, Nagasaki and Kobe, collecting signatures from the consulate in each location, to verify her progress. From there she sailed to San Francisco before finally making her way back to Boston, within the prescribed fifteen-month window.

To raise the $5,000 that formed the second half of the wager, she discovered a deep entrepreneurial streak within herself. She quickly recognised that a woman riding a bicycle around the world would attract attention, so she enlisted companies to pay her to ride with their names on placards on her bike. Her principal sponsor was the Londonderry Lithia Spring Water Company, which asked her to take the somewhat extreme step of changing her name to theirs. She changed her name! Imagine if Lance Armstrong had had to change his name to Lance US Postal Service or Lance Discovery Channel as part of his skeevy sponsorship deals! On the other hand, her given name was Kopchovsky, so Londonderry may have felt like an upgrade.

On her journey home through the United States, she engaged in speaking engagements, to raise the remaining funds and satisfy the bet. A true storyteller, sticking to the facts was less important to her than spinning an amusing anecdote, and she fabricated plenty. Tales of tiger hunts in India filled her lectures, along with an anecdote of narrowly escaping death at the hands of Asiatics who considered her an evil spirit.[2]

Annie was the first woman to circle the globe by bicycle, *on a dare*. Most of us eat caterpillars or worms on a dare. Sure, she didn't ride the whole way, and sure, she made up some of the grand tales she told in lectures, but the fact remains that she undertook a journey most of us can only imagine. She returned transformed both physically and mentally; her body

---

the century could reasonably handle. That is some seriously shit weather to deal with, so she did the sensible thing and headed back to New York.
2 She never went to India.

was sculpted and her mind was set on the potential of women. Upon her return home to Boston, she packed up her family and moved to New York, where she became a journalist focused on Women's Rights, writing under the byline 'The New Woman'.

Most of us are better people when we ride. Annie not only became a better person by riding but helped liberate women in general. Holy fucking shit, that's some perspective on our own meagre contributions right there.

BERNARD HINAULT

The Badger versus The Dog:
Paris–Roubaix 1981

Paris–Roubaix is bullshit.
Bernard Hinault

Think about this for a minute: Chris Froome winning Paris–Roubaix. Hard, nay impossible, to imagine? What about Vincenzo Nibali? Slightly more plausible, but still, if either of those guys were ever to line up in Compiègne in April, only the insane would give them a chance of taming the *pavé* and winning a sprint in the hallowed velodrome.[1] They are, of course, Grand Tour riders,[2] and these days those sorts of rider don't care much for spending a Sunday in Hell.[3] That is a key differentiator between the species of *rouleur* and *pretendeur*.

---

1 Pavé is the French word for cobblestones, presumably akin to 'pavers' or some such. There is a group in France called Les Amis de Paris–Roubaix whose function is to maintain, preserve and restore these ancient roads, so they stay just the right side of completely un-fucking-rideable.
2 The Grand Tours are the three most important stage races, each lasting three weeks: the Tour de France, Giro d'Italia and the Vuelta a España.
3 See Jørgen Leth's seminal Paris–Roubaix documentary of the same name. Also p. 53.

Let me in there, coach! Let me at him!

Bernard Hinault. *Le Blaireau*. The Badger. One of the last of the old breed who could win races over three weeks *or* one day. Specialisation wasn't really in his vocabulary. Racing was his only speciality, and he proved it by winning hillier classics such as Liège–Bastogne–Liège and Amstel Gold as well as five Tours de France. He was just one badass French mofo, who didn't care on what stage he crushed fools. So long as fools were being crushed, he was happy. Not that 'happy' was exactly his natural state. To this day he is portrayed as a bit of a bastard, which may or may not be accurate. But who's going to ask him and risk a punch in the head or being pushed off the nearest podium? No one, that's who. OK, maybe Greg LeMond. Doesn't matter if you're a striking, race-blocking dockyard worker or a flower bearer. The Badger still commands respect with those fierce, dark Gallic eyes and his stature, akin to some sort of stray

French mongrel bulldog. If Hinault *were* a dog, or even an actual badger (*le Blaireau* being his best-known nickname), he'd definitely be limping, missing an eye and ready for the next fight.

Paris–Roubaix, the Queen of the Classics, wasn't just a passing thought for Hinault, as some may think. He had previously finished fourth in 1980, behind a Who's Who of cobble-munching monsters: Francesco Moser, Gilbert Duclos-Lassalle and Didi Thurau. But 1981 would be his year. Sporting the World Champion's rainbow jersey he won at Sallanches, in his home country, may have provided extra motivation for Hinault. What better way to stamp one's authority on the sport than by winning in the bands?

Anyone who has ridden the stones knows how demoralising they can be, and how easy it is to be dropped in the blink of an eye. You don't have to be weakening to get dropped on the *pavé*; you don't need to be on an off day. You can be 100 per cent and still get dropped just for a moment's inattention or because you took the wrong line through the morasses and lost your rhythm. It's every man for himself, and you need to be a proper hard one if you want to play at the front end. The 1981 race was one of those magical editions of Roubaix where – and this is something that a generation of riders today have never seen and are reluctant even to believe – it rained. If you've ever ridden the *pavé* in the wet, or are one of those old sages that did get to watch a muddy Roubaix, then you'll also know just how much more shit it will make a rider's day. Hinault's day wasn't going so well, and a pissed-off Badger is bad news for everyone.

If you crash at Paris–Roubaix, you can be forgiven for calling it a day, crawling – broken – into the broom wagon, or trundling solemnly into the velodrome to get the finisher credit.[4] To finish

---

4 The broom wagon is the bus that follows the race at the minimum allowed speed. It lurks at the back, reminding everyone that if it passes them, they are then either going to be riding on alone, for pride, or

Maybe if I do some squats, I can win this race ...

this race is an accomplishment in itself. Crash *seven* times, and you'd be forgiven for crawling into a ditch and crying yourself to sleep or death, whichever comes first.

But Hinault didn't care much for broom wagons, or trundling. And he *never* cried. He dragged himself back into the race after each of his seven (that's V plus two) crashes, and found himself in an élite group of *klassiekers* containing no fewer than four previous winners: 'Mr Roubaix' Roger De Vlaeminck, Francesco Moser, Hennie Kuiper and Marc Demeyer.[v]

With the business end of the race approaching and the notorious Carrefour *pavé* safely behind them, it was on to the often underestimated *secteur* at Gruson, where the stones are smoother but slippery in the wet, owing to their blueness.[6] Rain

---

climbing into the bus for the journey to the finish, reflecting on how soft they are.

v *Klassieker* is the Flemish term for Cobbled Classics specialist. See Part III.

6 Honestly, their blueness makes them faster but also slippy. Blue means granite. The French. Just go with it.

had been falling most of the day, so the slickness of the *pavé* was something to be respected, as well as the ornery posse of badasses all around. Riding near the front, Hinault reached the right-hand bend that signals the end of the *secteur* and a welcome transition to smooth tarmac, when a black poodle – apparently named Gruson – jumped in front of the riders and took the Badger down, while RDV pulled off a piece of handling only equalled recently by Peter Sagan and managed to stay upright. Now, if this hadn't been Paris–Roubaix, and if Hinault hadn't been in the lead group fighting for the win, I'm sure fluffy little Gruson wouldn't have survived the wrath of the Badger. But he had a race to win, and in the time it took to say 'votre chien est mort' he was up and remounting, giving chase before the others could even get out of sight. The Badger was pissed off, again, and you know how *that* ends.

If you haven't seen the video of this race, we suggest you go watch it now to appreciate the task that lay ahead for Hinault. You done? Good. Pretty impressive, *non*? It was only a matter of a kilometre or so before he was not just back in the bunch but at the front, driving the pace, angered and no doubt plotting a trip back for a reunion with Gruson after he was done with those pesky bike riders. This is what separated Hinault from the rest: he could take a negative situation and turn it in his favour, and you could almost sense that his breakaway companions were defeated the moment he got back on. The look in his eye would've been enough to make them cower and think twice about even leading him into the velodrome. 'S'il vous plaît, après vous, Monsieur Blaireau.' It would come down to a sprint on the track, and Moser, RDV and Demeyer, in particular, might have fancied their chances in the velodrome. They should have known better.

Hinault recounts that he checked the wind direction blowing the flags as he entered the track, which shows how much of a thinker he was, despite the animalistic treatment he inflicted on his bike. Legs and heart and brains make a bike rider. Coming in second-wheel, he then took the lead and ramped up the pace, and, but for a brief poke of Demeyer's nose into the wind, Hinault led for the bell lap, with his rivals surely thinking he was committing sprinter's suicide by going so early. The pure V he laid down on the banking was formidable, and still amazes us to this day how simply and methodically he destroyed his rivals from the front.

No, we won't be seeing Froomey and Nibbles doing this ever, and it's unlikely we will see such all-round badassness again in our lifetime (or a wet Roubaix, for that matter). The Badger was a true *rouleur*, who knew how to rule, by his own rules.

MEGAN FISHER

Overcoming

There is something about Cycling and overcoming tragedy. Greg LeMond won the Tour de France after getting accidentally shot while out hunting, by his brother-in-law. (We wonder how that goes down at family holidays: 'Yes, Greg, we all think it's hilarious when you pretend *this* is the turkey John was aiming for.'[1]) So did Lance Armstrong, who may well have been a pathological liar and an asshole but he didn't fake getting cancer, and he didn't fake returning to the top level of the sport. Floyd Landis – another liar, but not nearly as much of an asshole – overcame a degenerative bone condition in his hip and still managed to ride into Paris with the yellow jersey on his shoulders.[2]

Meg Fisher is another such rider. At nineteen, barely out of high school, Meg was involved in a car accident that took the life of her best friend and the lower part of her leg. What it must be like to wake up to that reality, we can only imagine. Besides the

---

1 Greg's brother-in-law's name was changed in order to protect ourselves from having to research his actual name, which we assume wasn't John.
2 We recognise he didn't actually win the Tour de France in 2006. On the other hand, racing the Tour de France – let alone crossing the line first – with that kind of injury is quite a feat, irrespective of any drug use.

Breathing like a whale shark.

life that was lost, a future without sports for a gifted athlete such as her must seem an impossible world to face. Meg eventually decided she didn't need to live in such a world and that she had some choices. Notable among them were:

- Apply Rule #5
- Science the shit out of riding a bike with a prosthetic leg.

When we say 'Science the shit out of it', we mean loads of science, but also *even more* Rule #5, because it sounds like riding with a peg leg really sucked before she sorted it all out.

As she wrote on Velominati.com:

Fundamentally, I rode like someone who had an exceptional leg length discrepancy. When I rode with my everyday prosthetic leg, it lacked the biomechanics inherent in intact ankles. During a pedal stroke with an intact ankle, there is plantar flexion & dorsiflexion. Since I could not accomplish these movements with my prosthetic, I had to compensate by shifting on my saddle and changing my biomechanics everywhere. Observers could clearly see my hips and lower back shifting dramatically during every pedal revolution. I had to set my seat post height high enough so that I would not pinch the back of my left knee during the top of the pedal stroke. If my seat height was too low, I developed blisters on the back of my knee that could be so bad that I literally could not walk the next day. I also wanted my seat height low enough so that I could reach the bottom of the pedal stroke. Usually, people with a leg length discrepancy would not develop blisters on the back of their knee.

My prosthetists mounted the cleat under what would be my [left] heel. They also made the pylon a bit longer than my shin on my other [right] leg. These adjustments allowed me to reach the bottom of my pedal stroke and keep my seat height high enough to relieve pressure on the back of my knee. By using a specially designed cycling prosthetic, I became better able to keep my hips 'quiet' on my saddle.

It is true that Cyclists don't like walking very much, but I think we'd all agree that it is convenient to be able to do so should the occasion call for it. Lying on the couch moaning about your guns because of how hard you crushed it that day is one thing; lying on the couch with festering foot blisters is another thing altogether. But resolving the blister/pinching issue apparently didn't resolve the other issues: lower back pain, right knee pain and deep pain inside the front of her right hip that felt like someone was driving an ice pick into her joint capsule. In spite of this, Meg won her first pair of Rainbow Jerseys at the UCI Para World Championships (road race and time trial).

At that point a friend came up with the bizarre idea of shortening only her left crank arm. This is a major mindfuck for any able-bodied Cyclist, but it miraculously cleared up her symptoms and set her on the road to recovery. Meg has gone on to win nine World Championship medals (five gold, two silver, two bronze) on the road and on the track, in addition to the Paralympic time trial gold medal and pursuit silver medal.

Before her accident, Meg wasn't a Cyclist. In recovery she not only found a new life as a Cyclist but became an example for all of us. Cycling is already the hardest sport on the planet, only made harder by doing it with a peg leg. But it is also the most beautiful sport in the world, and perhaps the contrast of pain and beauty is what makes it so irresistible for those who truly need to overcome.

FRANCESCO MOSER

Passista

Moser was a classic *rouleur*, although, being Italian, he was really a *passista*.[1] He was – and is – a big, handsome northern Italian. Known as *Lo Sceriffo* ('The Sheriff'), he was equally deadly on the track, road and cobbles. He was one with his bike. Bent low at the hips, with a flat back and a powerful, smooth stroke. Poetry in motion. His *palmarès*: world road champion, Italian road champion, a handful of Monuments, the 1984 *Giro d'Italia*, stage wins and *maillot jaune* wearer in the Tour de France, the Hour Record. But it was his three (consecutive!) Paris–Roubaix wins that took him deeply into Hardman territory.

Italians who thrive in the Spring Classics of Belgium and northern France are few, but Moser was certainly one of them. His modern-day equivalent would be Fabian Cancellara, whose roots are in the mountains of northern Italy also. They are both tough guys on the bike and gentlemen off it. Both embrace new equipment and new technology. Both have the *rouleur/passista* willingness to power up to the redline and hold it there until the damage is done.

In the head-to-head comparison of Fabian and Francesco, Mr

---

1 Italian for *rouleur*; Moser is too Italian for French labels.

Watch me drop you in my little ring.

Moser still comes out head and shoulders above, in the broad, indefinable yet crucial 'I will dominate you and look fucking fantastic doing it' category. What Francesco Moser had in abundance, *abbondanza* if you will, and what most other Hardmen lack, was the grace and beauty that seem to come naturally to most Italians, curse them. None looked better at the finish line than Moser. The whitest of socks, a perfect kit. To look good is to feel good. It is the very distillation of the Velominati. Consider this account of a brush with greatness:

> Before the race began I walked into a portaloo, that most English of outdoor institutions. As I took a leak, I heard the clacking of shoe cleats on the lino and Italian voices behind me. I was aware of the pungent smell of continental liniment – a particular smell, a special smell that mixed expensive cologne with embrocation.
>
> As I looked down, rearranging the bloo cubes in the pisser, all I could see next to me was a pair of immaculately shaved brown legs, perfectly folded white cotton ribbed socks and perforated calf leather racing shoes. I really wanted to turn and stare but I froze and ran out to be greeted by the smell of fried onions and burgers. It was to be a day of contrasts.
>
> Camille McMillan, *Rouleur* magazine

Really, expensive cologne for a bike race … suddenly the feeling of inferiority to Francesco is even stronger (if that is possible).

A vivid demonstration of Moser's grace under fire is captured gloriously on 35 mm film in *A Sunday in Hell*, the classic, must-watch Paris–Roubaix documentary from 1976. The camera motorbike is on a dusty *secteur* of cobbles, where two French riders are trying to catch a four-man break. An unidentified rider flies past on the right. He is in a hurry. The moto catches up and there he is: *Lo Sceriffo*, resplendent in the Italian National champion's *tricolore* jersey. He is pure power and beauty as he surges down the right-side gutter. The two French riders are unable to get on his wheel. To see this is to understand who is a *rouleur* and who is not. Moser said Paris–Roubaix was harder than his Hour Record, and to see him racing on the cobbles is a paradox because it looks so entirely natural that one can hardly understand that any effort was involved at all.

While we civilians cannot be 'Cecco' Moser, and wearing

expensive cologne while riding might not work for anyone less Italian, his position is worth unabashed emulation. Riding with a flat back and horizontal torso is something everyone should strive for. Aerodynamic drag is your greatest foe and your body is the greatest transgressor in this department. Stop catching wind with your chest. Photos of Merckx, De Vlaeminck, Moser all show them with elbows bent, back flat, torso pulled low for maximum efficiency through the wind.

While we can't actually ride like Moser, we can try to imitate him and, in some way, flatter him, which doesn't end with his position on the bike. Don't dress like a rodeo clown for your next ride. Shaved tan legs would be nice and maybe a pair of crisp white Cycling socks, not too tall, not too short, like Goldilocks. That unfortunate tattoo on your leg – get that taken care of, as in, removed. Never desecrate the legs.

RIK VERBRUGGHE

Stage 15, Tour de France 2001

What, another Flandrian[1] has made it into *The Hardmen*? Get used to it. It is not our fault; they grow them up hard in Flanders. Rik Verbrugghe does not have the *palmarès* of some of his Belgian brothers, but any professional would be proud to have his. Verbrugghe's tenure at Lotto overlapped with Andrei Tchmil – Soviet-born but turned Belgian, as any sensible Hardman would. Rik joined Lotto as a neo-Pro[2] and had Tchmil, famously tough enough to reset his own dislocated fingers mid-race and carry on, as a teammate, staring him down across the breakfast table every day. (For more on Tchmil, see Part III: *De Klassiekers*.) Verbrugghe must have put this daunting experience to good use, however, and he surely channelled his inner Tchmil when he rode Stage 15 of the 2001 Tour de France.

Stage 15, which followed a rest day, was a sprinter's stage. The Tour coverage was all Lance and Jan, Jan and Lance.[3] The

---

1 A native of Flanders, Belgium, where even small children ride in the big ring.
2 A first-year professional. One who is now experiencing the abrupt transition to higher speeds and longer distances. And going from winning all the under-23 amateur races to finishing last, if at all.
3 Jan is Jan Ullrich. Who does not feature in this book.

We don't need no stinkin' helmets. Rik wins Stage 15 of the 2001 Tour.

climbing stages were all but done, so the non-*grimpeurs* were gunning for some glory. A lot of excellent *rouleurs* were working hard to make sure the day ended with a sprint. A large group battled off the front of the main field, and Marco Pinotti escaped in a long solo bid for the line. What followed was Rik Verbrugghe chasing off the front after Pinotti. Verbrugghe was both the hunter *and* the hunted. The footage from the TV motorcycle was awesome to behold. Their route went through shadowed woods, and there was something primal about this chase through the forest; predator and prey in a full-on pursuit. Verbrugghe was the lone wolf, Pinotti the fleeting deer. Verbrugghe's position was perfect; his low, flat back would have made Moser proud. He was flying! He kept the chasing pack at bay, just, and closed in on Pinotti, steadily. It was a breath-taking display of how fast a Cyclist can go, kilometre after kilometre, in search of his prey. His strength was rewarded as he caught Pinotti before the finish and handily beat him to the line in the sprint.

There is something about riding fast off the front of any group, even if that 'group' is merely your riding partner. Being chased, not getting caught, brings out that atavistic fear to stay ahead as if your life depends on it – that funny itch at your neck like the one you had when you walked up the stairs from the cellar when you were a kid, like something was behind you. It's good to reconnect to that feeling; it makes you want to get out and train more, work harder, to get used to the feeling that you can outlast whoever is chasing you.

While the 2001 Tour was all about the US Postal team's dominance, the Velominati came away with a different memory: that Verbrugghe, he is a Hardman, no?

BERYL 'BB' BURTON

British Twelve-Hour Time Trial 1967

Getting chicked: getting passed on the bike by a female. Let's get this straight: there are always going to be better Cyclists passing you, and many of them are going to be female. If you didn't get over this a long time ago, take a hard look at yourself and get over it now. Getting chicked as a professional is rare, as men and women do not usually race together. Most amateur Cycling events are segregated too, for better or for worse. But occasionally fate plays its hand and the women do get to play with the men. And when it happened in Yorkshire, in 1967, Beryl Burton was there to make history.

Burton, a pure *rouleur* if there ever was one, was not only competitive against the men; in this race she was better. We hope she wouldn't have taken exception to being classified as a Hardman.

To ease off would be the beginning of the end. It's a bit like packing[1] really. Once you have packed in a race it becomes easier next time, and so on, the rot sets in, it erodes one's self-discipline, and anyway, it's a negative way to race!

Beryl Burton, *Personal Best: The Autobiography of Beryl Burton*

---

1 Yorkshire for abandoning.

*Why put a little ring on your bike if all you're
going to ride is The Big Ring. Exactly.*

In time-trial-mad Britain in 1967, the twelve-hour national
championship was open to women. Why was Britain so mad for
time trialling instead of road racing? The Veclominati are unclear
but suspect it has something to do with everyone always driving
and riding on the wrong side of the road.

Why would one even hold a twelve-hour time trial? Because
there are enough nutters in Britain to compete in an event so
desperate. Burton was born for it. By the end of her career she
would have been a multiple world road race champion and
world pursuit champion. She was on the World Championship

pursuit podium twelve times over three decades. She held time-trial records for all distances, repeatedly improving them, accumulating close to one hundred racing titles. To overstate her *palmarès* would be impossible. And you can add to it: mother, full-time rhubarb farmer, homemaker and bike mechanic.

During the twelve-hour record Burton chicked Mike 'British Best All-Rounder' McNamara out on the course as *he* was on schedule to set a new twelve-hour men's record. He was the last of the men's starters and she was the first woman, so she became his two-minute (wo)man. Poor Mike McNamara, and we're not even talking about how 'cartoony' his name sounds. He started off faster than he had ever planned and stayed on the rivet for hour after hour to keep Beryl behind him.[2]

Their two-minute offset remained stubbornly even. But twelve-hour races do require the odd bathroom break, and eventually McNamara had to stop to answer a call of nature. Right after his long-put-off nature break, there she was. The thought bubble above his head? Something like 'Oh, for fuck's sake, here it comes, let the chicking be quick and painless.'

As she pulled alongside, they chatted briefly, then she applied the *coup de grâce* to his faltering morale by offering him a piece of liquorice. *Liquorice!* And then off she went, no doubt leaving a faint aroma of aniseed in her wake.

Her women's twelve-hour record stands to this day: 38.5 kph over twelve hours. To quote Sean Kelly: 'Jaysus.' Hardman really does not come close. To be the greatest female in a marginal sport like Cycling; let's just say she didn't have to worry about being too much in the spotlight. This was a fate Beryl Burton bore with her customary stoicism. While none of us is ever going to be as badass as Beryl, it should teach us that anyone just might

---

2 The old Brooks leather saddles were riveted together with one on the nose and several across the back. To be 'on the rivet' was to be perched on the front of your seat, going as hard as possible.

have something like that hidden inside them. If someone's son or daughter shows a passion for a sport, especially a sport you think they might not usually enjoy, don't hold them back. They could soon be catching yesterday's best and leaving them in their dust. Like a punk. It's what Beryl would do.

Beryl's life ended on the bike, but not in a way one might expect. She was out delivering birthday invitations for her fifty-ninth birthday and died of a heart attack. Too sad, and at the same time too perfect.

PART II
LES GRIMPEURS

When I attack, I try to psychologically destroy my rivals, who never know how far I can go … it's hard to tackle a mountain when you know the suffering that's around the corner.

Marco Pantani (1970–2004), *Rouleur Magazine*

Riding a bicycle is like activating a superpower. When we ride, we almost fly. We are suspended above the ground, gliding along at speed. Our velocity depends on how much we can summon from our mind, body and spirit. Few sensations in life are as seductive as that of the strength in our legs as we accelerate up a rise in the road, controlling the intensity of our effort.

That feeling of strength gives way to a certain tension as our climbing effort continues and our muscles begin to fatigue. Fatigue leads to weakening, then actual pain: a taste of the suffering to come, should we choose not to heed these early warnings. Climbing is the easiest way for us to suffer on a bicycle; gravity does its best to ensure that every pedal stroke is met with the cruel reality of physics. The higher we climb, the greater the cruelty of its pull. To make matters worse, the higher we climb, the thinner the air. With every pedal stroke, our muscles are weakened and our lungs deprived of a little more precious oxygen.

Steep climbs strike fear into the Cyclist. Steepness means suffering. On gentler gradients we can choose how deeply we want the pain to cut; these climbs will hurt plenty only if we attack them at speed and keep heaping coals on the fire. But a savage gradient offers no choice at all. The suffering is total. We are forced to pour all the power we can find into our pedals in order simply to stay upright. When the Power Well runs dry, we turn our hopes to the sweet baby Jesus in the form of whimpering grunts and hopeful wails. We all know 'forlorn hope' isn't exactly a strategy, but it certainly starts to look like a great plan when your only other option is climbing off the bike.

The problem with dismounting on a climb is that it makes quitting feel acceptable; we accept not being good enough. The capacity to quit and then continue our lives as though nothing has changed is unique to the human species. This is a lesson that we must unlearn. The reality is that nothing worthwhile lies at the end of an easy road; struggle leads to triumph over the impulse to quit. Lance Armstrong said, 'Pain is temporary; quitting lasts for ever,' proving that even assholes can be insightful.

Climbing is the most unnatural thing we can do on a bicycle; the pull of gravity and the weightiness of even the lightest among us means that The Witch with Green Teeth is constantly tugging at our jersey, holding us back as we ascend.[1] The best climbers exert monumental control over the impulse to make the suffering end. This is the species known as *grimpeur*, and while we may never understand what twisted instinct it is that compels them to seek out and embrace the worst kind of pain, we can empathise with them every time we pedal laboriously up the local wall, stoic in the belief that we are Climbing Well For Our Weight, mimicking as best we can our Alpine heroes with hands in the drops, dancing on the pedals (Moonwalk not recommended) and attempting what we pass off as 'attacks'. To onlookers we are just guys and girls going slowly uphill on bikes. But inside our hearts, lungs, legs and minds we are burning with all the fire of Bahamontes or Pantani on L'Alpe d'Huez. In those horrible moments when the summit seems never to come, we are all *grimpeurs*: the kings of suffering.

---

1 The Witch with Green Teeth is the French equivalent of The Man with the Hammer: she lurks in the shadows and swoops in to cause a sudden and catastrophic failure in the engine room.

LUCIEN VAN IMPE

The Spotted Flandrian

Should it surprise us that the best pure climber, ever, would come from the flatlands of East Flanders? Perhaps it shouldn't. Lucien Van Impe was born into Cycling (three of his uncles were professional racers) in 1946. Five foot six, and with the physique of a mid-'90s supermodel, he was not ideally built for the constant battering winds that harden riders from Belgium, where the wind is your constant training partner. The only kind of wind they have in Belgium is a headwind, and it is there to make sure you stay low over your bars. It demands extra force on the pedals, always. It locates your weakness. It separates you from your riding partners and makes you ride home alone as punishment for your inadequacy. But how does that help you climb?

Of course, it doesn't, apart from making you accustomed to endless, fruitless suffering. But climbing just came naturally to LVI; a Flandrian upbringing taught him everything else. By the time he turned Pro, he knew how to crouch low over the bike and power across the landscape. And he could hold his own in a time trial – often a weakness of climbers.[1] In fact, if the course

---

1 We are thinking specifically of someone whose name shouldn't really even be uttered in an article about Lucien Van Impe, that someone

was hilly, he could excel at it; he managed to beat fellow Belgian Eddy Merckx by almost a minute in a 40 km individual mountain time trial in the 1975 Tour de France. But it was his work in the high mountains that really got him noticed.

The ink was barely dry on Lucien's first Pro contract – he was in just his second day as a professional – when he started the 1969 Tour de France. There was none of this talk of holding the young guy back for a few years before racing his first Tour. You are from Flanders? OK, you are already tough enough. Indeed, he *was* tough enough. He finished twelfth in his first Tour and was third twice, fourth and fifth between 1971 and 1975. Those are placings of a true Grand Tour contender considering these were the Merckx years, where everyone was racing for a podium position because the top spot was already taken. Merckx's Tour wins were like Lance Armstrong's dominant reign, minus the dickish behaviour. Riders and the public became bored and even a little resentful of Eddy winning Grand Tour after Grand Tour. So while Eddy was monopolising the *maillot jaune*, Van Impe was busy collecting King of the Mountains polka dot jerseys.[2]

---

being Andy Schleck – a gifted *grimpeur* who could have won the Tour de France if he could have been arsed to improve his time-trialling. If ever anyone trained his strength instead of his weakness, it was he. Is there a word in Luxembourgish for anti-Hardman? It would sound like 'Schleck'. There are support groups for those few unfortunate individuals afflicted with 'Dirty Schleck Love', who still somehow admire him. Some of the Velominati have been seen leaving these support groups, collars upturned, stealing into the night.

2 The polka dot jersey, the dotty jumper, for the leader in the King of the Mountains (KOM) contest in the Tour de France, is awarded daily, but he who wears it at the finish in Paris wins the overall best climber's title. This is a very controversial competition, since it can be won in a calculating fashion, even by a modest climber, if they are single-minded enough. It is awarded on the collected points attributed to each climb – rather than timings or stage wins – so a rider can go out early in the Tour and collect enough points to lock up the King of the Mountains even before all the Alps or Pyrenean climbs are over. Chief offender is

In 1976 two things broke in Lucien's favour: Merckx was unable to start the Tour de France, and Cyrille Guimard became Van Impe's *directeur sportif*. It was Guimard who saw the opportunity for overall domination if he could motivate Van Impe to aim for the yellow jersey instead of the spotted one. And that is a tougher transition than one might think. Pure climbers don't win the Tour de France: to fight it out for the polka dot jersey means a focus on mountain stage wins dotted along the three-week race; winning the Tour de France overall means shifting the focus from a dozen key stages to performing perfectly day after day for three full weeks.

Cyrille Guimard deserves credit for many riders' development. He was a recently retired racer, still in his twenties, with a mind focused on innovation. If ever there was a sport mired in tradition, it was Cycling. The bikes, the clothing, the food, the training, all mostly unchanged for decades. This is how it was done and how it shall be done. 'Continuous and sublime recapitulation', as that blind old monk in *The Name of the Rose* put it, though perhaps not with road racing in mind.

Guimard had new ideas. Each of his riders needed to be personally coached and their equipment optimised. He was the guy who began raising saddle heights: the showing of post began with him.[3] LeMond said he was the best coach he ever had, and even the extremely stubborn Breton Bernard Hinault did *some*

French pretty-boy and seven-time KOM winner Richard Virenque, who understood how to accumulate the needed points, despite his chronic lack of V. You can read more about him in his own section, on p. 91, not that he really deserves it.

3 The amount of seat post exposed above the seat tube: as in 'that dude is showing some serious post'. This *need* to show more post has resulted in half the Cycling public with their saddles being much too high. Cyclists tend to overdo everything, so if showing some post is good, then showing a lot of post is better, obviously. The temptation is to keep showing more and more post until you are crippled with saddle sores and you hit car park barriers with the small of your back.

of what Guimard told him to do, because Hinault understood Guimard would force him to become a champion.[4] Luckily, Van Impe was under Guimard's tutelage also. Guimard was tactically astute, and his recently retired status meant he intimately understood the cast of characters out on the road.

Van Impe was issued orders first through a teammate and then through an assistant director to attack on the next col. He resisted them both. The next thing he knew, Guimard had stormed up in the team car, hand planted firmly on the horn, threatening to run him off the road if he didn't attack there and then. Guimard kept on at the reluctant *grimpeur*, and by the end of the day Van Impe had put enough time on everybody to say he had the Tour de France won, even though there was still another week to go before the finish in Paris.

> His ability to accelerate in the high mountains was just enormous. He could beat anybody in a mountaintop finish and was able to win the Tour on his climbing skills alone. That's something you can't say about Virenque.
>
> Cyrille Guimard

Finally, it must be mentioned, Lucien Van Impe looked amazing on the bike; awesomely strong, tanned legs, crisp white socks, snug jersey. He understood the importance of Looking Fantastic at All Times. His *souplesse* on the steep cols was enviable.[v] He even – and this may never have been achieved before or since (Cipo certainly failed at it) – looked awesome, with some sort

---

4 Guimard once said: 'In terms of pure physical capacity Hinault was the greatest Cyclist ever, If he'd trained like Eddy Merckx, he would never have lost a race.' Obviously the Breton did not do *everything* demanded of him.

v *Souplesse* is smoothness, nimbleness, suppleness, specifically of pedalling. Another example of fantastic and translation-resistant French Cycling language. The development of *souplesse* is a lifelong vocation.

*Belgians and frites go together more
than Belgians and climbing.*

of Belgian perm going on up there. Luckily this happened late in his career, but it did burn a lasting impression into a young Velominatus' imagination.

Had Lucien Van Impe not had Guimard offer to run him off the road, he would never have won the Tour. And we should take heed of this. Do we, too, need someone behind us, leaning on the horn and yelling? Yes, because however tough we may be, we often need an external factor to help us burrow ever deeper into the Pain Cave. They are doing it because they see what we can do better than we ourselves can see it. Has a Cycling mate ever baited you into a ride you thought was over your head? And you survived? It turns out some of your friends are pretty damn wise, at least when sober.

STEPHEN ROCHE

La Plagne, July 1987

Grimpeurs are a select lot. They possess a maddening ability other Cyclists simply don't have: they can change their climbing tempo from 'too fast' to 'way too fast', repeatedly. Fellow *grimpeurs* can trade blows, attacking each other, recovering, attacking again until only the pure climbers remain. If a non-*grimpeur* is baited into playing this dangerous game, they will lose by going so far into the anaerobic zone that they crack badly and end up losing handfuls of minutes. Non-*grimpeurs* simply shouldn't get drawn into that fight. They need to ride at a tolerable but steady tempo and accept losing some time and places to the pure climbers. This rule holds true all the way from the Grand Tours down to the café ride between friends.

Stephen Roche was a fantastic all-round rider, a great time trialist and a decent climber. But the difference between a decent climber and a great climber, like his rival Pedro Delgado, can be decisive in a Grand Tour. The final stage of the 1987 Tour de France, Stage 25 (that's a lot of stages!), was an individual time trial. Delgado was only moderate against the clock, so Roche calculated he could make up about a minute's deficit on him in that stage. But no more.

The Colombian pure climbers had been busy schooling the

Sometimes, you just have to put it in the big dog.

Europeans in the mountains that July in 1987. Colombia must have more climbs than descents in it, because they tend to be rubbish descenders. On Stage 21 Delgado, Roche and Charley

Mottet worked together on the descent of the Galibier, to distance them. They understood that they had to shed the Colombians before the day's final two climbs, the Col de la Madeleine[1] and final up to La Plagne. Roche, not wanting to duel Delgado up to the mountaintop finish, attacked way out, before even the Madeleine. It was a bold move. He soloed all the way up and down the Madeleine. And yet it was a bad move, as Delgado and teammates caught Roche in the valley before the climb of La Plagne. Advantage Pedro.

Part-way up La Plagne, Delgado began his attacks. Stephen knew that following Pedro meant certain defeat. With his lesser climbing abilities, it would be like bringing a spork to a gun fight. So he let him go and dug in hard to limit his losses. He could not dig hard enough, as Delgado's advantage kept growing. It grew past that one minute Roche thought he could get back on the final day's TT. The Tour was steadily slipping out of his grasp. As the gap stretched out to one minute and twenty-five seconds, Roche asked for a bigger shovel. If he could dig in here, he knew the last five kilometres were not as steep and maybe he could take back some of Delgado's advantage.

There were no radios. The mountain was enshrouded in thick, heavy cloud. Visibility was virtually nil. The information on time gaps was non-existent. The stage winners were already up the road. Delgado knew he had to bury Roche as fast and as deep as possible, and he was doing just that. Between the crowds, the noise and the sinuous road neither man knew where the other was, just that one was ahead and the other was behind, with the Tour win somewhere in between.

Roche passed the '5 km to go' sign and went on the attack.

---

1 How much trouble can a climb be, when it is named after a delicious cookie? Spoiler alert: it can be vicious. In fact, probably the more delicious the name of a climb, the more ferocious it is. Beware any climb named 'beignets'.

If anyone was going to bury Stephen Roche, it was going to be himself. He rode like a demon. He knew, as a time trialist, as the terrain eased, if he could get his speed up he could hold it for a few kilometres. This is where Stephen Roche earned his Hardman status and performed the deeds of a *grimpeur* despite not truly being one. With a kilometre to the finish and Delgado still up the road and out of sight, Roche reached down with his left hand and put the chain on to the big ring, the Big Ring, dear reader![2] *No one* anywhere on La Plagne had his bike in the big ring. To be clear: he had already raced up the Galibier and soloed the Madeleine, only to be caught and dropped by his rival on this last climb. When Roche went *sur la plaque*, as the French call it, he nearly stalled to a stop. Other riders passed him thinking, Roche, that lad is in a spot of bother there. But he got that big gear turning over and started to eat up the road like a junkyard dog eating a T-bone steak.

On the final short straight to the finish, through the mist, Roche saw Delgado ahead, just crossing the line. One minute twenty-five had been reduced to five seconds. Past the line, Roche looked like death. He was ashen. You can't go that deep, for that long, and not pay an awful price. He was pulled off the bike and laid down on the ground, looking very bad. The medics administered oxygen, covered him in a foil blanket and whisked him into an ambulance. In the ambulance the oxygen brought him back to life. His blue eyes showed a little sparkle. When asked how he was feeling, he said, 'Everything's OK, *mais pas de femme ce soir*.'[3] He left the mountain in the ambulance, which is not the ideal way to exit a day's racing. But leaving the

---

2 AKA *la plaque*, the big dog, or, if you are an old school Flandrian, your only chainring. Why would you ride in the small ring? You would just go slower.

3 'But no woman for me tonight.' An Irishman who speaks French. Naughty boys, the lot of them.

race in an ambulance with a quip like that? Well now, that's different.

If we ever end up in the back of an ambulance in our Lycra, would we be ready with an old-school line when the paramedic pulls off the oxygen mask and asks how are we going? Probably not, and if we did, they would think we had brain damage. And there would be no media to record the moment's excellence. Still, it would be excellent.

Lucien Van Impe counselled that climbing was an art that could be learned. But he was a natural, so what does he know? The civilian Cyclist *can* learn to become a better climber, but we should not be crossing swords with the real *grimpeurs*. Stephen Roche showed that a *rouleur* can learn to climb just enough. And when even that is not enough, a Hardman should simply put it on the big ring and push on the pedals. And that really is the lesson here, for all of us: go big; leave your mates shaking their heads, just once in a while. What got into him today?

Riding sensibly, staying out of the red zone, not hurting yourself … it's all overrated. What's the worst that can happen? OK, besides ending up in the ambulance. And even if that happened, it's your big chance to drop your Stephen Roche line. There is no reason *not* to really hit out on the bike once in a while. Who knows? It just might work.

MARCO PANTANI

Les Deux Alpes

'My pain is self-chosen; At least, so The Prophet says.'

Layne Staley, Alice in Chains, 'River of Deceit'

We expect our heroes to suffer; in fact, we *demand* that they do. But we don't necessarily appreciate the depth of that suffering. What we witness on the television screen shows little of what they are really going through: the fluidity of their motion creates an illusion of effortlessness. It is only because we have also ridden a bicycle, and therefore suffered, that we can achieve at least *some* understanding of what the Pros' efforts feel like.

When the Pros crash, more often than not they jump to their feet, gather up their machine and sunglasses, leap back onboard and crack on, as though the incident upset their rhythm but little else. In fact, every crash hurts. There is no cure, there is no remedy, there is no getting used to crashing so it sucks any less. Have you come off recently? Yes? It sucked quite sharply, didn't it? No matter how cool they make it look, it is just as bad, or worse, for our dear heroes. (Remember, they're probably going a tiny bit faster than us.)

Our heroes are human, after all. We tend to forget that. We

imagine them to be hardened, somehow immune. Steeled against the dangers that lie along the day's racing *parcours*. But they face the same risks as we do when they climb aboard their bike. In fact, they are as vulnerable to impact with tarmac as we are. And they are also just as vulnerable as us to poor morale, self-doubt and bad judgement. Racing a bicycle professionally doesn't make you perfect, no matter how great it looks from down here in the peanut gallery.

Marco Pantani was more artist than athlete, his brilliance matched only by his crippling self-doubt. When all the pieces came together in the right order, he was unstoppable, seemingly making molehills of mountains as he tapped out a relentless rhythm in his distinctive style. He didn't spin the high cadence we see in modern climbers but instead rode bigger gears, typically out of the saddle with his hands in the drops instead of the more common position on the brake hoods. His style was graceful and elegant, yet powerful; every time he felt his rhythm wane, he rose out of the saddle and poured a few more watts into the pedals.

To this day Marco holds the two fastest ascent times up L'Alpe d'Huez, despite going off-course on one occasion. He set those times at the end of full mountain stages with L'Alpe as the final ascent. Not even a freshly blood-transfused Lance Armstrong could match either of those times on a 14 km time-trial sprint up from Le Bourg-d'Oisans to the ski village above Huez.

Pantani's legend is full of amazing feats, but his greatest moment was in the cold, pouring rain from Grenoble to Les Deux Alpes during the fifteenth stage of the 1998 Tour de France. He had targeted this stage because it passed over two of the most obnoxious passes in the Alps: the Col de la Croix de Fer and the Col du Galibier. The Croix de Fer ('iron cross') is a terrible pass; halfway up, just as you settle into your rhythm, it ascends sharply to avoid a dammed lake before descending back to where the pass would naturally have continued on. If

Today, we pray to our Prophet, who art in Belgium.

you have ever ridden a long mountain climb, you will know how demoralising it is to lose all your hard-fought elevation for something so random as a damned dammed lake. The Galibier, on the other hand, is just high, cold and brutish. This is a climb that goes relentlessly into the clouds, and just as your suffering reaches its maximum potential you pass by a gated tunnel that, were it open, would give passage to the other side of the col and its welcoming descent. Instead, the road churns on and on up to the faraway col.

Pantani, in '98, languished far down in the General Classification, and it is unclear whether he had any designs left on the podium in Paris. But he wanted this stage, and our hero, who should have been immune to race-day nerves like us mere mortals, was so gripped by his anxiety that he fell off on one of the hairpin turns on the way up the Croix.

He attacked from the base of the Galibier, in the pouring rain. Rarely has a rider Looked So Fantastic climbing a mountain: head wrapped in a bandana; his sunglasses, rendered useless in such conditions, perched atop his head; his face steeled, showing effort but not suffering. He was a machine that day. Over the top of the Galibier, between the ever-present glaciers, Marco struggled to get his rain cape on. He pulled over and stopped, losing valuable seconds rather than risk crashing or freezing without protection. Sometimes the difference in the race is measured by the precautions one takes, not the risks. Those precious seconds were repaid by a faster, warmer descent into the valley, where Pantani flew up the final climb while his rivals – including the race leader, Jan Ullrich (who hated racing in the cold and wet) – lost large chunks of time. Ullrich finished more than eight minutes behind, handing the *maillot jaune* over to Marco. They battled all the way to Paris, with Marco prevailing, to become the first Italian to do the Giro–Tour double since the great Fausto Coppi.

It's no secret that, despite all his imperfections and indiscretions, Marco Pantani remains one of our very favourite riders. Not just because he rode uphill faster than anyone ever, not only for his style and composure while in lactic acid hell, nor for Looking Fantastic at all times despite being blessed with some big ol' ears and premature baldness. It was more the fact that for all his brilliant athleticism and God-like celebrity, he was real, and vulnerable, and flawed. Just like us.

ANDY HAMPSTEN

The Gavia, 1988

It's a sign of how rich our sport is that some of the most heroic rides in Cycling history go virtually unmentioned. Not necessarily spectacular victories but deeply impressive feats, drawn from deep in a rider's physical and mental reserves. There is no better example than Andy Hampsten's ride over the Gavia in the 1988 Giro d'Italia. Riding a Huffy. It wasn't actually a Huffy, but instead a bike made by famed American frame builder John Slawta, of Land Shark, but it said Huffy on it and we all know you're not allowed to lie in writing. Growing up in the States, Huffys were for kids, and even by our childish standards they were crappy bikes. At the time we imagined Hampsten's bike was heavy and felt like spaghetti and meatballs on wheels, and had a coaster pedal-brake.

Hampsten had found some success in the professional world in 1985, when he won Stage 20 of the Giro while on a one-month contract with Team 7-Eleven. Hot on the heels of that success, Bernard Hinault snatched him up and brought him into La Vie Claire as a mountain goat *domestique*.[1] But by 1987, 7-Eleven

---

1 'Mountain goat' is a term we use to describe that annoying breed of Cyclist who insists on going uphill much too quickly for everyone else, the annoying little twunts.

Hey, guys! If we go fast, we'll stay warm!

was in search of a new leader, having sacked Alexi Grewal on account of his consistent violation of Rules #36 and #37, a lifetime commitment to violating Rule #43 and his highly questionable headgear choices.

The 7-Eleven management did not panic when they awoke on the morning of the stage to find it was cold and raining in the start village and to hear that over a metre of snow had fallen high up on the Gavia. Many of them, being based in Colorado or in the American Midwest, knew a thing or two about snow and promptly bought up all the cold-weather gear they could find in the local ski shops and made plans to distribute it to the team's riders along the route. It's fortunate that the management had some inkling as to the ordeal they were in for, since it appears the riders were fairly oblivious:

> On the way up I got rid of all of my warm clothes, my legs were bare, no shoe covers. I did have a pair of neoprene diving gloves that I kept on for the entire climb. Along the way my team car gave me a neck-gator and a wool hat.
>
> I wanted to dry my hair before I put it on maybe 4–5 ks before the top, so I brushed through my hair, thinking I was going to wipe some water out, and a big snowball rolled off my head, and down my back.
>
> I thought, 'Oh my gosh, I'm really not producing much heat, even though I've been going up a really hard grade.' So then I had my raincoat, a super-thin polypro undershirt on, so my arms were covered, but I was NOT warm at the top of the mountain. We could spend a few hours while I figure out how to describe how cold I was!
>
> Andy Hampsten, as told to *Pez Cycling News*

Up was cold, but tolerable. Down was excruciating. Those of us who have descended a mountain on a sunny day know that going down is much colder than going up. Those of us who have done it in the cold or rain know that your body gives up on mere shivering and moves on to full-body shakes in an attempt to stay warm. Chaos ensued. Hardmen wept. Riders stopped at the side of the road and pissed on their hands and legs in a desperate attempt to warm their extremities. The Dutchman Erik Breukink flew the coop and won the day, but the big winner was Andy Hampsten, who went on to claim the only American Giro d'Italia win to date. More than that, though, he claimed a place in the all-time Hardman ranks owing to that ride, and a legacy that only seems to grow the older it gets. Cyclists now appreciate weather conditions by asking themselves the question 'It's cold out, but is it *Hampsten Cold?*' If the answer is no, then see Rules #5 and #9 and get your ass out training.

NAIRO QUINTANA

Rule #9 Grimpeur

Colombia produces great *grimpeurs*. It must be something in the water, or the coffee, or the air. Actually, it's probably in the non-air, busily not-existing in all those high Andean passes. Lucho Herrera infiltrated the European peloton back in the 1980s and started to pull on a *lot* of dotty jumpers. Other Colombians followed, and the peloton had a fight on its hands in the mountains. Who were these guys, and why were they so good at going uphill? And why did they always come off, going downhill?

Colombia has a lot of kids on bicycles, good weather and plenty of altitude. Nairo Quintana, now Columbia's undisputed Cycling superstar, commuted to school on a bike, over bad roads and a 3,200 m pass. Respect. He won the Tour de L'Avenir, the amateurs' Tour de France, at the age of twenty. At twenty-three, in his first Tour de France, he was second to Chris Froome in Paris. It was the best placing in the Tour for any Colombian, ever. This was Big. Back home, kids were eschewing the bus for a bike by the thousands. The following year he won the Giro d'Italia.

In 2015 the Tour de France was going to use part of the route of Paris–Roubaix. To prepare properly, Nairo toed the rainy Belgian start lines of E3 Harelbeke and Dwars door Vlaanderen,

If your legs still work, you didn't go fast enough.

to feel the cobbles at race speed. He was out of his comfort zone, but he wasn't put off. In fact, the wee little Columbian seemed to like it:

> I feel good in this country, I enjoyed it and I think I'll come back ... In the future, I'd certainly like to come back and do Paris–Roubaix, even though it's obviously not a race that suits me ... My sensations on the cobbles were pretty normal. Sure, it was something different but I felt very good on them.

A *grimpeur* who wants to race Paris–Roubaix is not your average *grimpeur*. And Quintana thrives when the weather goes to hell too. Professional Cyclists, skinny bunch that they are, don't always handle wet and cold all that well. But it brings out the best in some. Vincenzo Nibali, from *Sicily*, mind, is one such rider, and Nairo Quintana is most definitely another. We saw proof of this on Stage 16 of the 2014 Giro: rain in the valleys, sleet on the slopes and a full-on blizzard up on the mountain passes. The race went over the Gavia and the Stelvio and finished on the Val Martello.[1] This stage was a *grimpeur*'s delight; not a flat kilometre to be seen, three huge climbs but two huge descents, every kilometre ridden in rain, sleet, snow or fog.

Descending a cold mountain at race speed in soaking-wet kit: it is the worst. Everyone needs to experience it once. To do it twice in one stage? Leave that to the professionals. Riding up in the sleet and snow looks hardcore, as we see in many classic Cycling photos. Not so many great images of wintry descents, are there? The photographers can't even hold their cameras to their faces.

In 2014 confusion over a possibly neutralised dangerous descent helped Quintana get into the *maglia rosa*.[2] Communications between race officials, *directeurs sportifs* and riders became muddled as the race approached the final snowy descent of the day. Some thought it was neutralised, and some did not. Some stopped and put on extra layers, some didn't. And it could be that the Giro's race officials should not have been using Twitter as their main communication method. After all, Twitter lacks

---

1 The Gavia and the Stelvio are two famous and extreme passes in the Dolomites. One of the Gavia's ascents looks like a paved goat path. The Stelvio is the classic ribbon of loopy switchbacks carved into the face of a mountain. In the best of weather they are both a real handful. When the weather turns bad … well, just ask Andy Hampsten. He's probably still shivering.

2 Usually, the very beginning of a race is 'neutralised' as it leaves a busy town centre. This means everyone rides behind the race commissar's car until the signal is given that the real race has begun. To neutralise a race after it has officially started is rare; since when are terrible weather, terrible roads or terrible spectators an excuse to stop a bike race? So when race organisers do try to neutralise a race in the middle, confusion reigns. The *maglia rosa* is the leader's jersey for the Giro d'Italia. It carries the same significance as the Tour de France's *maillot jaune* but is arguably better looking.

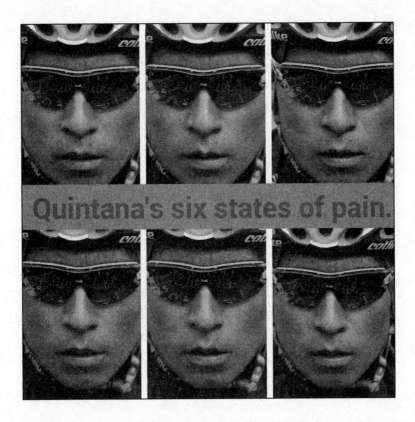

the hand and arm gestures required for Italians to communicate properly. The fact of the matter is: Quintana didn't waste time before the descent to stop and pull on a rain cape like even a certain big-eared Italian *grimpeurino* would have; he just descended like an ox, dropped his breakaway companions and soloed to the mountaintop finish. The climbing and descending of multiple wet, snowy Dolomite climbs, dropping whoever is still with him: that put Nairo in the *maglia rosa*. So apparently when you're Colombian and you are somehow a great descender as well, then you win Grand Tours. A fact that Nairo confirmed with his 2016 Vuelta title.

Unless he's bluffing (and he does have a good poker face),

Quintana gives the solid impression that riding through rain, sleet and snow bothers him very little. It is just like riding to school, right?

RICHARD VIRENQUE

Cracked Actor

If he hadn't been a bike racer, Richard Virenque could easily have been a French film star. His swarthy good looks and lean body, piercing dark eyes and smooth-as-silk voice would have served him well as a crime-fighting action hero, a French James Bond who's done a lot of hard drugs. But just as some good guys turn bad, so this prodigal *grimpeur* son of French Cycling went from hero to villain and just as quickly back again. That said, many still demonise him to this day, particularly those parts of the population that aren't French, or *les femmes*, or both.

Even to include Virenque in this book was a divisive and controversial choice. While all of us enjoyed watching his exploits in the Alps and Pyrenees during the Golden Age of Bad Old Days at Le Tour, some of us now hold him in the sort of esteem we also reserve for the likes of Armstrong and Rumsas.[1] While all those guys were doping, Lance and Raimondas were also being bullies

---

1 Raimondas Rumsas was a solid Lithuanian Classics rider who made the tell-tale miracle leap to Tour stardom with a third place overall in 2004. It may have had something to do with the car full of drugs his wife was busted with at the French border. Like all good men, Rumsas blamed the women, trying the old 'my mum has a heavy period' defence, but to no avail.

I don't know about your jersey, but I love the shades.

and coercing others into doing some nasty deeds on their behalf. In that respect, Tricky Dicky's biggest crime seems to have been crying on television while trying to blame everyone else for the

Festina Affair, for which he was made the poster boy. (We won't describe it all over again. If in need of illumination, please see any other Cycling book, ever. Or Google.) A faded, ripped and dog-eared poster, sure, but still a poster, and Virenque liked to be looked at. But denial is the first line of defence for every doper who ever got popped, or looked like getting popped, or was nowhere near getting popped but *Goodfellas*-helicopter-scene-paranoid they were gonna get popped. So his tearful performance may have grated with those who were tired of hearing it all before, and the addition of the waterworks was one step too far. 'This bloke should've been an actor!'

Now, you don't ride up mountains faster than most, win stages, wear yellow multiple times and win seven polka dot jerseys without being just a little bit tough. Once Virenque had sat out his weepy penance and made his return to the Tour, he not only had to battle his rivals, the press and half the fans, but also his biggest adversary: himself. Coming back as a clean racer only made things that much harder, so he didn't. OK. Disclaimer: we don't really know if he did or did not continue to medicate upon his return, but, armed with hindsight of the era he came back in, we wonder whether Monsieur Virenque was riding *paniagua*.[2] The best evidence of this came not in the Alpine stages he won post-holiday but in a ride he produced on one of the flattest, most sprinter-friendly *parcours* on the one-day race calendar: Paris–Tours.

Bunch sprints and Virenque have never been included in the same sentence, ever, until just then. Whatever the motivation was for him even to line up at the 2001 race, to get in a breakaway and to have the slightest chance of winning belies logic. Climbers don't have much to gain at Paris–Tours, unless they're on some tempting appearance money deal and just need to get on

2 Spanish term for 'bread and water', as in riding without medical enhancement.

camera for an hour or two. Virenque could have slipped into that role easily; there was no way a break would be allowed to stay away, so all he had to do was flash the pearly whites, slick back the un-helmeted hair a few times, wave and blow a kiss to the housewives when they finally swept him up (the chasing peloton, not the chasing housewives).[3] There'd be other riders to help maximise the TV time, so why the hell not?

But no one else came. Virenque jumped away from the peloton after only 12 km, and would have expected to be joined by at least a half-dozen companions. But no one came. No one except the archetypal suicide breakaway merchant Jacky Durand (see p. 32). A climber and a dreamer. The peloton relaxed and let them go, knowing they would be seeing them again in a couple of hours or so. Maybe they didn't remember Dudu's win in Flanders nearly a decade earlier, or were too young to know, or perhaps believed that such a feat couldn't be achieved twice. And Virenque, well, he'd not be much use to Durand in this situation either. On they pedalled, kilometre after kilometre peeling away, building up a huge eighteen-minute buffer to the chasers with only 60 km raced. There were still almost 200 more to go. This'll be sweet, thought the peloton. Rain and cold descended on the cruising pack, so they upped the pace to keep themselves warm and get to the finish a bit quicker. They'd catch the escapees soon enough.

Bike racers on the whole aren't very good at maths, which is why they have *directeurs sportifs* to do all that thinking stuff and yell it at them through the radio in their earpiece. Ride harder, ride slower; it's basic stuff really. With our hero's lead now whittled down to thirteen minutes, the confidence in the bunch

---

3 Virenque, despite possessing Fantastic French Hair and with the compulsory helmet rule still two seasons away, instead chose to wear a *casquette* (a cotton cap – the most revered of Cycling headpieces). In a disgraceful display of decidedly non-French style, he chose to wear it *backwards*. It was his biggest, and probably only, mistake all day.

would've been rising. We've got this, lads, no need to worry. Further it fell, to seven minutes with about 70 km to go: piece of cake. Andrea Tafi, the swarthy Italian cobble-muncher, tried to get across to the breakaway with three others, and came to within four minutes of the French dynamic duo but no closer. Meanwhile, Durand was beginning to look more like the Robin of the outfit, and started to weaken as the outskirts of Tours loomed ever closer. Batman meanwhile had been looking after himself better and decided he didn't need a spent and complaining Boy Wonder holding him back. Ten kilometres to the finish, and now only fifty seconds ahead, with two short climbs to go, it was death or glory time. Virenque chose the latter and finally freed himself from Durand on the penultimate climb. Four kilometres to go, twenty seconds lead. The peloton eats that up in a k, let alone four.

Well, it didn't work out that way. Not for the peloton, or their mathematical advisers, or whoever should have been telling them to 'ride harder'. At just 2 km to go, Virenque had a slim fifteen seconds. 'Reechard' buried himself to within an inch of crying on the flat Avenue de Gramont and, on his final look behind, saw that his six-hour stint at the front of a flat race that he wasn't supposed to win was about to pay off. And this is when he committed the sin that we believe re-buried his reputation in the eyes of many: an elaborate finger-kissing, arm-raising, poignant-French-yelling salute. He would repeat that obnoxious multi-gesture for the rest of his career, but only on mountain tops, where at least he, if not it, belonged. But in many respects Virenque's Paris–Tours coup was the greatest, most emotional and meaningful win of his career.

TYLER HAMILTON

The Accidental COTHO

People hate needles. Hypodermic ones that is – we're sure your grandmother still loves her six-inch double-points. No, we're talking skin-piercing, intravenous instruments that only junkies look forward to seeing regularly. Even though they don't really register on the pain scale once they've pierced the skin, most victims – or 'patients', to use the medical industry's terminology – will still cringe and tense and turn to face away from the source of the impending stabbing. And looking the other way is something that professional Cyclists are well versed in.

Tyler Hamilton knew this better than most, as he'd tried to do it for his first couple of years in the Pro peloton. But he soon realised that the things he was trying to ignore couldn't be ignored or avoided. Things like, say, organised doping on a colossal scale. Accept it, do it, but pretend it doesn't exist. Question no one, answer nothing. We now know this as *omertà*.[1] From

---

1 Originally applied to the Cosa Nostra, this code means silence, non-cooperation with authorities and non-interference in the illegal actions of others. It has become pelotonspeak for *see no evil, hear no evil, speak no evil*, while actually being pretty damn evil. Hamilton's book *The Secret Race* describes how everybody within the sport knew what was going on, but never acknowledged it except by the act of actually doing it. There

virtue, honesty and pride to vice, deception and shame, Hamilton's transformation, like that of every other rider who has travelled the doping path, was invisible to the naked eye, or at least to those eyes looking in from outside the sport's inner sanctum. Sort of like the Masons, isn't it? You know there's something dodgy going on, probably involving sacrifice and possibly blood, but all you get to see through the crack in the door is a couple of old guys who look like your own gramps playing a game of cards.

What was always in Hamilton, long before his first red egg or jab in the ass, was his Hardman genetics.[2] Those who knew their Cycling could see that this quiet, affable lad knew how to absorb pain to a level that even Gewiss-level juicers could barely handle.[3] He not only endured the suffering; he welcomed it, relished it. Pain, both physical and mental, rode pillion on Hamilton's entire career, and beyond.

Once that new-dog-in-the-pack innocence had been carefully removed from Hamilton's psyche, as it had with hundreds before him, it was replaced by what is known as the COTHO phenomenon.[4] Most who suffer from this terrible affliction display an

---

was one guy who flaunted it, though, almost taunting the media and the governing bodies to catch him if they can. They could, eventually. Dickhead.

2 A 'red egg' is a little red candy-like pill which is actually testosterone. Sounds delicious.

3 Gewiss was a team infamous for experimenting with the blood-booster EPO under the guidance of doping mastermind Michele Ferrari, who famously declared that EPO was no more dangerous than orange juice. Gewiss routinely went 1-2-3 in races throughout the season.

4 COTHO: oft-quoted acronym, which doesn't *quite* stand for Chap of the Highest Order. Originally applied to a certain Texan, it spread throughout the annals of the Velominati and has been applied to many other pedigreed dopers who display a certain, er, *chappiness*. Doping alone is not a sufficient qualification for COTHO status; a true COTHO will display other classic traits such as being Texan, riding a Trek, possessing beady blue eyes that are way too close together and being named Lance. Being a dick in general is also a qualification.

alarmingly similar pattern of transformation. Talented young rider wins national titles, steps up to small-time Pro team, gets good results, gets picked up by major team, gets hammered by a pack of juicers, vows to beat them by honourable means, can't beat them, inevitably joins them, becomes a COTHO. Hamilton didn't really look like a COTHO, or indeed a rider with any discernible killer instinct. He looked more like a doe-eyed boy, too small and frail to be taken seriously as anything other than a good lad who will carry your shopping then mow the lawn and trim your hedges, ma'am, all for a glass of cold lemonade. But just as heroin or meth can turn handsome straight-A scholars into haggard petty thieves, so hanging out with the wrong bikie crowd can set a good lad on a path of destruction. As they say, you hang around dogs, you get fleas.

Now we all know the stories of how Lance would intimidate and control everyone around him – even teammates who had given loyal, unquestioned service to help him to his biggest wins – then discard them like last night's IV drip. Hamilton managed to avoid his inevitable fate longer than most, but he must have known it was coming. When? Well, no one could predict the unpredictable Pharmstrong. What was different in Hamilton's case was that his career would profit rather than suffer from the COTHO-by-association status he had acquired. With his move to be leader of the CSC team he was now his own Hardman, not a lackey for the neighbourhood bully boy, no longer working for lemonade.

Liège–Bastogne–Liège is the oldest of the Spring Classics and is the big prize for the men with no chance of survival in the fields of Flanders or on the Roubaix cobblestones; it's for the *grimpeurs*. If there was ever a Classic made for Hamilton, it was this. In 2003 it was pouring with rain, and he attacked at the perfect moment, with everyone looking around, not wanting to chase because he wasn't a likely threat. But he was the sort of rider who found it all too thrilling to suffer like a dog, so he gave it the beans all the way to the finish line. As he came within sight of the line, he checked behind him to survey the threat of chasing riders; the video clearly shows his disbelief that none was within reach. In that moment, he went from super-*domestique* to dominator, and it gave him the boost to take a genuine shot at his old boss on his turf: at the Tour. Under the tutelage of the *directeur*-formerly-known-as-the-greatest-doper-ever, Bjarne Riis, he had at his disposal the backroom smarts and well-stocked medicine cabinet of the notorious Mr 60 himself, and he was a willing patient of the team doctors.[v] (Are they really doctors, or are they just play-acting, like Dr Nick Riviera in *The Simpsons*?)

Fresh on the heels of his win in Liège, Hamilton started the 2003 Tour de France as a hot favourite for the overall victory. Things didn't go to plan when he took a tumble on Stage 2, breaking his collarbone; he soldiered on with the injury, not only taking a glorious stage win in the Pyrenees in south-west France but coming fourth overall in the general classification.

Now, we're no experts on the ability to suppress pain, but we'd be willing to bet that, riding for three weeks with a freshly broken collarbone, grinding your teeth to stubs owing to the pain (which he did) and occasionally pissing blood (which he also did), you'd need something a little stronger than a tablet or two of Ibuprofen to cope with it all. And we're also pretty certain, when we witness someone not only riding for three weeks with a cracked clavicle but also attacking, winning stages and battling for the podium without so much as a grimace, that something deeper than just a good poker face is being deployed

---

v The blood-boosting drug EPO increases a person's red-blood cell count, or haematocrit. If used unsupervised, this can lead to a dangerous thickening of the blood. Medical studies have shown that a healthy person's haematocrit should stay below 50 per cent in order to avoid danger. Bjarne Riis, was known as 'Mr 60' for his willingness to boost his blood all the way up to 60 per cent. And boast about it.

OK. I guess that qualifies as a grimace. Case closed.

here. Whatever it is that can do *that*, we want some. What's that? It's called *grinta*? We're pretty sure you can't get that down at the drug store.

PART III
DE KLASSIEKERS

The thing about the cold is that you can never tell how cold it is from looking out a kitchen window. You have to dress up, get out training and when you come back, you then know how cold it is.

Sean Kelly, Irishman of legendary toughness

Many of us found our way into Cycling by chance. A fateful intersection between life and the bicycle that changed us for ever. In 1980s America there was little TV coverage of this largely European sport, so the only races we had heard of were the Tour de France and Paris–Roubaix. Three weeks of racing over the plains and mountains of France matched against one brutal day of racing on roads built by the Romans and Napoleon (and maintained, shall we say, 'Frenchly' since then). These were the two known ends of the European bicycle-racing spectrum.

We devoured issues of *Winning* and *VeloNews* magazines; their arrival, months after the races they covered, was hugely anticipated. Sometimes a stray copy of a French or Dutch magazine would somehow infiltrate our group of riding mates and be passed around. These magazines were largely incomprehensible to us, but the photographs in their pages provided all we needed to cling on to an entirely new level of devotion to and passion for the sport, as we devoured every last detail of races we hadn't even known existed.

Of all these races, the Spring Classics, in particular, stood out. Perhaps for the simple fact that the riders looked like they had just returned from another century, having taken up arms in some long-forgotten war between bicycle and road. The photos showed the strongest, most hardened Cyclists in the world, covered in mud and blood, their faces fractured with grimaces of agony. And of all the Spring Classics, Paris–Roubaix, in particular, known as The Hell of the North, was by far the most brutal.[1] The roads were savagely rough,

---

1 'The Hell of the North' is the semi-official nickname of Paris–Roubaix, originally because of its route through war-ruined Belgian landscape, latterly perhaps more because of the back-from-the-dead expressions on the faces of the finishers.

including several *secteurs* of unforgiving *pavé*, and the timing of the race in early April meant the conditions were often atrocious, with rain filling the air and mud covering the already treacherous road surface.[2]

What exactly makes the Classics so special? In short, they are a collection of some of the most beautiful (partly because they're so ugly) one-day races on the calendar. They are old – many of them are a century or more old. And they are steeped in myth and legend. Some of the Classics, such as the Giro di Lombardia and Paris–Tours, take place in the autumn, and some of them – most notably the Ardennes Classics – are defined by short and steep climbs.[3] And not all of them take place in northern Europe. But the most sacred Classics to the Velominati are those contested on cobbled roads in Belgium and northern France in the springtime.

The Flemish population of Belgium – Cycling nuts, all – consider the cobbles to be their private domain (including Paris–Roubaix, despite the inconvenient fact that it takes place in France and not Belgium). And there is no higher praise for a rider than the word they reserve for a specialist of the cobbles: a *klassieker*. The *klassieker* is a special kind of rider: hearty of nature, so not easily prone to illness or injury. One who loves cobblestones, rain and wind, in part because others dread them. Many *klassiekers* start their careers as

---

2 *Secteur* is French for 'sector'. *Secteurs* are typically short in length, usually anywhere from 1 to 3 km. It is customary for the amateur Cyclist to shout 'SECTEUR' at the top of their lungs upon entering a section of *pavé*. This is to disguise what they truly want to shout, which is more likely to go something like 'OH SWEET BABY JESUS, PLEASE DON'T LET ME SHIT MYSELF!'
3 Paris–Tours: an odd little race, a typical Sprinter's Classic which was somehow won on one occasion by twiggy French climber Richard Virenque and inexplicably never won by the greatest Cyclist of all time, Eddy Merckx. In fact, it's the only major race Merckx failed to win. On one occasion he gifted the victory to his loyal teammate, Guido Reybrouck, then somehow never got another chance to win. No good deed goes unpunished, it seems. We should consider the possibility that Eddy doesn't lose as much sleep over his 'imperfect' record as we, his disciples, do.

sprinters before their youthful speed matures into sustained power and endurance and these long, tough races become their chosen domain.

The *pavé* that is the *klassieker's* natural home is brutal to cycle over. It is like riding two jackhammers at once; one you hold with your hands, the other with your butt. Eventually you accept that you are not controlling either, merely offering directional suggestions. It comes down to generating a lot of power and having faith that the bicycle will somehow keep pointing in the direction you're riding, which it always does, except for when it doesn't, at which point you find yourself suddenly lying in the gutter.

Maintaining momentum on the cobbles requires a massive engine; every cobble seems to hit your wheels like a boxer punching a bag. In order to maintain speed, the rider has to be constantly accelerating against these blows. And *actually* to accelerate requires a herculean effort. During the 2016 Paris–Roubaix Belgian *klassieker* Tom Boonen lost his momentum in the last corner of the Carrefour de l'Arbre – a long, cruel, slightly uphill section of cobbles deep into the finale of Paris–Roubaix where the race gets serious – he had to muster every ounce of his power simply to regain his lost speed.

Another crucial element of riding the cobbles is rhythm; if you can find a cadence somehow in harmony with the cobbles that are throwing your bike around, then suddenly you fly. If you are out of that harmony with the stones, every single turn of the pedals is a struggle.

In the rain, the cobbles are even harder. Particularly the bits between the *comparative* smoothness of the central crown of the *secteur* and the gutters either side. Here the cobbles are off-camber and treacherous. But what *really* makes cobbles hard is mud. We like to call it 'mud' because it goes in your mouth and it feels less scary when we call it 'mud' instead of shit, which is actually what it is, at least mostly. It goes in your mouth, certainly, but it also gets into every moving part on your bike, clogging your drivetrain and pedals, and stopping up the brakes. Over 250 km this added resistance will transform the pretender into a whimpering puppy, begging for mercy.

Our *klassiekers* are no pretenders. They are the real thing. They are the hardest riders in the hardest races, and we salute them.

ROGER DE VLAEMINCK

Mr Paris–Roubaix

It is a well-established fact that everything in the 1970s was 70 per cent more Awesome than in the modern era. The men were more studly, the women more studettely and the Cyclists harder and better-looking, all by a margin of 70 per cent, than men, women and Cyclists today. That's why it was called the '70s.

In this era Roger De Vlaeminck stood out as possibly the biggest heart-throb in Belgium, the most heart-throbby of the Cycling heart-throb countries, with only Eddy Merckx as a possible contender for the crown. His style, both on and off the bike, was impeccable. Hitherto only one man had ever tried to pull off the leather-trench-over-Cycling-kit look, and that man was Fausto Coppi. Roger was undeterred and styled the combination out without even trying, mitts and all. You can see the amazement registering on the face of the unhip bloke to his side, overleaf.

There are four documented cases where women required medical attention after observing him stroll by in a trim wool suit and skinny tie, but all four cases remain sealed for top-secret Male Sexiness Research. We don't want the results of the studies finding their way into the hands of the enemy, after all.

Many have postulated that Roger dabbled in performance-enhancing sideburn practices, although he has always

Sebastian! Hand me my cloak!

maintained that they were all-natural, and were enhanced by legal, over-the-counter oils and the odd tear collected from his vanquished foes.

De Vlaeminck was the quintessential *klassieker*; although he raced all year round (as was customary in his era), he always focused on the Classics in general, and the Cobbled Classics in particular. His speciality was Paris–Roubaix, which he won four times – a record that stood for more than three decades until it was matched by Tom Boonen in 2012. Roubaix is a race so hard on equipment that most of the wheels used by a team are thrown on to the rubbish heap as soon as it's over. RDV, however, rode the stones with such finesse that his wheels were simply serviced and put back into the working rotation for the team.

De Vlaeminck didn't leave his fitness to chance: he liked to train to the point of exhaustion, to build up his power and endurance to superhuman levels. His custom in the week leading up to Roubaix was to stack up a day or two on the bike of around 430 km, presumably drain a keg or two of malted Belgian recovery beverage and consume half a cow in prime ribeye. Then he was ready to crush the souls of his 'rivals'.

Hardman.

LIZZIE DEIGNAN

A Lady for the Sport

Sorry, I didn't realise I was going fast already.

There was a Dutch rowing champion who competed in the double for the Netherlands at the World Championships in the 1960s. After winning by more than a boat's length, he earnestly remarked to the press that it surprised him that, at a race of such importance, the other rowers didn't pull a little harder on their oars. It is an uncommon champion who wins so casually they genuinely wonder whether the competition is trying or not.

The 2016 spring Cycling campaign must have felt that way for Lizzie Deignan (née Armitstead), winning every important race on the women's European calendar. On the cobbles, on the gravel, in the hills. She won solo, she won in small groups. She waited, she attacked. Whatever the circumstances required, she met them. At Omloop Het Nieuwsblad she simply rode away from the group she was in, hardly noticing that she was riding fast already.

Making a living as a professional athlete is hard, especially in a fringe sport like Cycling. As men's Cycling has matured, it has slowly developed into a lavishly, if erratically, funded and *comparatively* well-managed sport. Media coverage has grown and with it sponsorship and supporting infrastructure. Women's Cycling, on the other hand, is at roughly the same level of maturity as men's Cycling was in the '70s and '80s, when riders largely managed themselves and drove themselves and their kit to the start of races. People come up with all manner of excuses not to support women's sports: the competition isn't fierce enough, the speeds are too low, the athletes aren't strong enough. Whatever correlation people have tried to find between having the ability to bear children and to compete at the highest levels was put soundly to rest at the 2012 Women's Olympic Road Race, which was an order of magnitude more Five and Nine *and* an order of magnitude more exciting than the men's race.[1] Lizzie was in the crucial move and eventually rode to the silver medal behind a nearly unbeatable Marianne Vos (see Vos section on p. 21).

A Brit taking the first home medal of the Games was a landmark achievement, and one that had the potential to change Lizzie's life for ever. But when the microphones were stuck in

---

1 Five and Nine: shorthand for Rule #5 (Harden the Fuck Up) and Rule #9 (If you are out riding in bad weather, it means you're a badass. Period).

her face at the finish, she didn't talk about what it meant for her as an athlete. She didn't talk about how huge an achievement it was for her. She didn't talk about her trade team. She didn't talk about her sponsors. She didn't thank her mum, or her family, or British Cycling. Lizzie talked about how the women had shown the Olympic Road Race the respect it deserved. She talked about the fact that it was a much better race than the men's race, and that women's Cycling deserved to be covered by the media and to be properly funded and supported by the UCI.

Women's Cycling *does* deserve better coverage and, since that day in July 2012, has started to get it. Change always happens more slowly than we would like it to, and it almost always requires an agent to set it into motion. Queen Lizzie saw the opportunity and sacrificed her own immediate agenda for that of her sport at large. It takes courage to speak out about the hard issues and risk humiliation on the world's stage. That day Lizzie Deignan showed bags of courage and became a powerful spokesperson for her sport. For that, we doff our caps to her.

GILBERT DUCLOS-LASSALLE

Never Say Die

I am made for this race. But does she want me?

Gilbert Duclos-Lassalle

When we watched Tom Boonen come within a whisker of beating Roger De Vlaeminck's record for the number of wins at Paris–Roubaix (four – see p. 107), we thought that the end was nigh, the last chance saloon had closed and the hands of Father Time had finally beaten him into a cruel submission. It's not how the script was meant to play out. Injuries had been battering his thirty-five-year-old body every season, but Tommeke – as the Belgian faithful know him – kept battering back twice as hard. But for the dream being snatched out of his grasp by (an even older rider) Matt Hayman, his thoughts might have been on kicking back rather than kicking on. A few minutes later, he probably thought of Gilbert Duclos-Lassalle.

Unlike our modern-day hero, Duclos wasn't a dominant Classics rider but a solid one. He'd twice finished runner-up in Roubaix, to Moser and Kuiper in 1980 and 1983 respectively, and came fourth in 1989. The rest of the time he was lurking in the top twenty and top ten of both Roubaix and Flanders, but

Hurry up, moto! I'm coming through!

it was a long time between drinks until 1992 rolled around. At thirty-seven, he was probably seen by the peloton as a regular feature, like the uncle who keeps turning up at Christmas every year but never brings any presents. Still, Duclos had a dream – not of a croissant and a coffee with his feet up, but of lifting a cobble in the infield of an old velodrome in a nondescript French shithole.[1] And he tried it seventeen times.

Seventeen years is a long time to be doing anything, especially something that is not guaranteed to end in any form of success or glory. Like accounting. Or plumbing, even, which

---

1 The winner of Paris–Roubaix gets a granite cobblestone on a plinth. Lifting it is quite a workout for a Cyclist's traditionally feeble, Mr Burns-like arms, which have additionally just been shaken halfway to destruction on just such cobbles. But neither the town of Roubaix nor its velodrome, where the race ends, is any kind of oil painting.

shares with riding Paris–Roubaix the unavoidable certainty of getting covered in shit. It must have seemed to Duclos that the 'Queen of the Classics' really didn't want him but somehow kept tempting him back. Like the ageing lothario who eschews the veterans' club for the disco, Gilbert kept his hair neat and kept turning up for one more dance. Maybe he still had it; maybe this dance would be the one. Always playing hard to get until she could resist his insistence no more, the Queen finally capitulated to Duclos. His 1992 Roubaix win was a climax probably more of euphoric relief than pure pleasure. That's what happens when you're old and you've been sitting on a bike seat most of your life. But it happened. Duclos-Lassalle simply rode away on his own and created history as the oldest-ever winner of Paris–Roubaix. Surely now, in the last year of his thirties, he would depart, with the final circuit of the velodrome a lap of honour, arms aloft, battered but not broken, a true champion leaving at the pinnacle of his career.

If Tommeke *had* won his record-breaking fifth cobble in 2016, he probably would have called it a day right there in the sacred temple and been blessed by the holy water that flows inside the consecrated catacombs, where they would carve his name in bronze for those who follow to venerate for ever.[2] And that would have meant going out in style. Duclos could have done the same, right then and there in '92, after winning solo, with no one else in the photo, the most beautiful way to win. Why risk another public beatdown from an old craggy lady in her nineties? And yet risk it he did, the very next year. It seems the obsession with this race, the aura or the mystique, keeps pulling until it's physically impossible to do it any more. He returned in 1993 to win by millimetres over Franco Ballerini in a thrilling photo finish. The old dog used his track experience to overcome the much

---

2 Which is to say, 'in the concrete shower block of Roubaix velodrome, where the winners' names are printed on little brass plaques'.

younger and overconfident Italian, who assumed he'd won and freewheeled for several laps with his arms waving about in the air before being given the news that he was, in fact, making a fool of himself.

Gilbert Duclos-Lassalle rode his last Paris–Roubaix at forty-one. He finished in nineteenth place. No one even notices the nineteenth place arriving at the velodrome. The showers are already filling up when nineteenth comes in at Roubaix, and the last of the hot water has already been used by the greedy guy who came eighteenth. This may be complete nostalgic bullshit, but to go out like *that* is probably even more honourable than quitting after a win. No fanfare, no pomp: just a man who quietly went about his business, who showed the utmost respect for all his nemeses and who, deep down, had only love and reverence for his career-long tormenter, whom he'd tamed but then given another chance to knock him back down a peg or two. Deep down, that's exactly how he understood the hierarchy worked – that no matter how good you are and even if you've tasted victory, the cobbles always win in the end.

JAN RAAS

The Dutch Make Hardmen Too

Even from a continent away, we North American Velominati understood Jan Raas was a badass. Every photo showed him hunkered over the bars in a hairnet,[1] glasses, muddy and plainly drilling it.[2] He was a Hardman from the Netherlands. He won the Dutch Amstel Gold race five times, but he understood that the Ronde van Vlaanderen was the greatest, toughest race there is.

An overview of his *palmarès*: world road race champion, national road race champion three times, Paris–Roubaix, Milan–Sanremo, Ronde Van Vlaanderen, twice. He had that devastating paring of talents: extreme hardness and a good sprint. He was hard enough to get over the short steep climbs again and again, hard enough to make every selection in the pack, so if a sprint was required after 270 km, he could win that sprint.

---

1 Not quite a helmet, and offering a *bit* more protection than a cotton cap, the hairnet was made of leather and stuffed with … something. It looked badass, full stop. Did it protect skulls? Let's just agree it looked badass.
2 Pushing hard on the pedals, crushing it, ripping the legs off, nailing it, on the rivet, *à bloc*, full gas, in the red, beasting it (UK only), majorly suffering (Sean Kelly only).

The Velominati would argue he is the greatest male Dutch road racer ever to throw his leg over a bike (the title 'greatest Dutch road racer' goes to Marianne Vos, *bien sûr*). And it's for his presence and attitude as much as his race wins. Sean Yates recounts the ritual of post-Tour de France criteriums where every day meant another drive to another race, and you were only paid if you finished.[3]

> Jan Raas was the king of the criteriums in Holland. As a former world champion and a serial winner of sprints in the biggest races, he held maximum respect and nobody moved without his say-so. His legs were notched, veiny, bulging and leaner than anything I'd ever seen, and he was a figure of great admiration for me. I remember a young rider called Teun van Vliet, who would become friends later, going up to Jan in the changing room before a kermesse [the Dutch term for criterium, also used in Belgium] with his hand up like a school kid.
>
> 'Please, Jan, can I win today? Please?'
>
> 'Flikker op.'
>
> Sean Yates, *It's All About the Bike*

Yeah, *Flikker op*, youth. I'm not driving half the night, eating at highway rest stops and getting four hours sleep, day after day, *after* racing three weeks straight at the Tour, just to hand you a race. Fucking earn it.

Here you have it, sports fans, genus Hardman in his natural environment. Jan Raas on his red and black TI-Raleigh steed, resplendent in the World Champion's jersey, thin leather gloves, hairnet. His black shorts are just barely containing the Guns

---

3 Criteriums are exhibition-style races held in provincial towns around France after the Tour. Traditionally, more emphasis is put on the big stars being visible and the local hero somehow winning than on strict sporting ethics. Deals are done, alliances made and results contrived. We wouldn't quite say it's the Cycling equivalent of WWE, but ...

This is what Awesome looks like.

of Navarone as he climbs. We are surprised the crowd is not plugging their ears as those guns go off. To add to his awesomeness, he had custom glasses with holes drilled around the outside to de-fog them better as he crushed fools in the cold, wet Spring Classics. We are beholden. Let this photo be a reminder that champions looked like this before they looked like Chris Froome. This is what a champion should look like. While Froome inclines toward low weight in the all-important power:weight ratio, Raas is doubling down on the 'more power' side of that equation.

A bad crash in the 1984 Milan–Sanremo damaged the temper of his hardness, and he retired from racing the next year to become a very successful director and manager. We cannot imagine that he suffered any fools or accepted any excuses of weakness from his teams.

Yes, my glasses have holes drilled in them.
What have you done today?

The last word on Raas goes to the young, still amateur Belgian Edwig Van Hooydonck (see next page), recalling a visit from Raas in an interview for *Rouleur* magazine:

Superconfex team manager Jan Raas came around his house to sign him for his all-star Dutch squad. The family always ate spaghetti after a race, so the Classics great joined them. 'We were all nervous, even the dog.'

EDWIG VAN HOOYDONCK

'Eddy Bosberg'

The Velominati's Keepers of the Cog gravitate towards the tall and too tall, so we like a lofty rider. Belgian prodigy Edwig Van Hooydonck was almost too tall to be a *klassieker* or Hardman. At 193 cm (6 foot 4) he was more spinnaker than sail, built to play centre for his school's basketball team – assuming people play basketball in Belgium – but, thank Merckx, he became a Pro bike racer instead. In the final analysis, there's no right height for the bike. It is all about how much heart and strength you have in order to turn the cranks. But still, the legendary bike builder Ernesto Colnago had to braze up a specially designed frame for him.[1] The standard-geometry 61 cm steel frame of the day would have been too whippy, so Ernesto made a more compact frame with an extended head tube and seat tube for the young maestro.

Team manager Jan Raas smartly gave Van Hooydonck his first Pro contract, with his Kwantum team, straight after EVH's win in the under-23 Ronde van Vlaanderen. In fact, Edwig rode Colnago machines for Raas's team for his entire professional career. That is a combination one needn't mess with. He won

---

1 Brazing up is an artisanal frame-building technique. Anyone in a bike shop with a beard or tattoo sleeves will be able to explain it to you.

both his Ronde van Vlaanderens the same way, earning his nickname: Eddy Bosberg. His approach (perfect for a non-sprinter):
stay at the front, keep the pace very high over the second-to-last
berg, then attack so fucking hard on the last one – the Bosberg
– that no one can follow.[2] Then power to the finish, solo. Simple
enough, and everyone would do it if they could.

In his first Ronde win, in 1989, he had on some bad legs,
which was good. It made him behave, conserve and let others
attack. As the rain and cold started to wear down others, he, as a
proper Belgian Hardman, started to feel fantastic. He floated up
the preliminary climbs, including the Muur van Geraardsbergen, as Raas, who knew a thing or two about winning the Ronde,
counselled restraint; wait, you must wait. He waited until the
Bosberg. And he was ready.

> In the winter of 1988, Van Hooydonck devised an austere
> training routine. He would drive to the Geraardsbergen house of
> Superconfex *directeur sportif* Hilaire Van der Schueren and do five
> laps of the Muur–Bosberg race finale … It meant that he knew every
> cobble by rote and these bergs held no fear.
>
> Andy McGrath, *Rouleur*

In a long race with numberless steep, cobbled climbs, the Muur
Geraardsbergen is often the crux. It is the cruel combination of
long and steep; many a Ronde has been won on it. In Edwig's day
the Geraardsbergen was the penultimate *berg* and the Bosberg
the final one. Edwig attacked on the Bosberg with such ferocity,
all the way to the top, opened a morale-ruining gap, put his head
down and kept that gap to the finish.

---

2 *Berg, hellingen, côtes,* and *muurs*: the abrupt, steep-to-very-steep, often
cobbled hills found in Belgium. These are usually found unexpectedly
after a quick right or left off a main road; there it is, oh fuck, a cobbled
ramp disappearing up, up, and up.

Note extended head tube for more Awesome.

This first Monument win, at twenty-two, in the cold rain, was everything a Belgian kid could dream of. Tears of pride on the podium overcame him. Belgium had its new hero and hung on his shoulders the heavy mantle of 'the next Merckx'. Van Hooydonck was no cannibal, but there never would be another Eddy.[3] Edwig went on to win a second Ronde in 1991 in exactly the same way, on the Bosberg. At the bottom of the Bosberg there was Van Hooydonck, Johan Museeuw, Rolf Sørensen and another rider from Sørenson's Ariostea team whose name would require research in order to recall. Again Van Hooydonck put in an attack

---

3 Cannibal: Eddy Merckx's nickname, which he himself apparently dislikes. And yet, if a rider in your generation has to be called 'The Cannibal', you'd rather it was you than your rival, right?

so fierce that he snapped the will of the other three and rode solo to the finish.

Here is where Edwig Van Hooydonck earns true Hardman status. The 1990s were when EPO's effects first rippled through professional Cycling. There were a number of unexplained deaths of healthy young Dutch Cyclists as the new drug was being experimented with; Cyclists were dying at night, their blood too thick with red blood cells to be pumped. It was not a banned drug then, but Jan Raas told Edwig not to touch it and he didn't. Eventually, everyone on the Ariostea team was staying on Edwig's wheel all the way up the Bosberg. Johan Museeuw, a known quantity, was beating Van Hooydonck regularly. The reason was obvious. And Edwig decided that *that* was not racing. He hung up his bike in 1996, not yet thirty years old.

It's a hard, hard man who wins the Ronde as a under-23 amateur rider, then as a twenty-two-year-old professional and then again at twenty-four as a favourite. Van Hooydonck doesn't want to be known as the Cyclist who retired early rather than dope. He should not have to be associated with doping at all, as he refused to do it. He should be known as a tough rider, easily one of the best Belgian racers of his generation. He walked away from Cycling, as a Belgian, as a multi-Ronde winner with still so much more to do. That was a real Hardman move.

26

SEAN KELLY, PART I

Guns

Sean Kelly was born with sprinter's legs. But mere sprinter's legs were not enough for him. Through willpower and sheer hard work he developed a pair of time-trialist's legs, climber's legs, cobble crushing legs and babe-magnet legs.[1] They didn't look like the legs that would crush many dreams, but they were.

The photo overleaf is reputed to be from the 1984 Liège–Bastogne–Liège podium, which Kelly won. Only a Cyclist would know these are Sean Kelly's legs. There are other legs more veiny, and there are legs with more impressive quads. But rest assured, these legs mean business. Eight days earlier they had won Paris–Roubaix, and the two races are not often won by the same rider. They amassed fifteen victories that spring. These legs could do it all.

---

1 We Cyclists always refer to our legs as a separate entity: 'I didn't have good legs today'; 'I had bad legs for the first four laps then they got better.' Ryder Hesjedal, the first Canadian winner of the Giro d'Italia, when asked about his form in between brutal Alpine stages, replied, 'The legs are mint!' Imagine different pairs of legs hanging in the mechanic's truck. They are installed before the race without the racers being told which model they have on. Having good legs or bad legs on any particular day is one of the great unsolved mysteries remaining in Cycling, as well as an effective smokescreen for your poor fitness, if used sparingly.

These are the sort of guns you have to tape down.

King Kelly won this Liège–Bastogne–Liège by enlisting Belgian friend and ex-teammate Claude Criquielion to help chase down Laurent Fignon and Phil Anderson in the closing kilometres and then winning a five-up sprint right on the line. Those legs always had a sprint left in them. As Kelly stomped his way through that spring season, besting everyone again and again, it was the grey duct tape on his shoes that left the impressionable Velominati so in awe. Tape. Why the tape? What did Kelly know that no one else did?

There are at least two plausible reasons for the tape on Sean Kelly's shoes, but first, a little background on toe straps: they sucked. They were archaic technology, seemingly a throwback to medieval knight's armour. A combination of a spring-steel toe clip and a leather strap with metal buckle to attach foot to bike. For them to be effective they had to be uncomfortable. More effective meant more uncomfortable. Getting into or out of them required bending down to tension or release the strap.

In Kelly's day all Cycling shoes had a cleat on the sole. The cleat had a slot, which captured the rear cage-plate of the pedal. The toe strap was then pulled tight across the top of the foot, holding the shoe's cleat down firmly against the pedal. The strap had to be snug all the time, and when things were about to get rough, Cyclists would be seen reaching down to pull them tighter.[2] Was this uncomfortable? Yes, of course. Did Sean Kelly care? No, he did not.

Back to the two theories on the tape. Theory One holds that the grey duct tape was there to protect his shoes from damage from the strap and buckle. Well-brought-up boys from County Waterford don't just waste expensive shoe leather. These shoes have to last all season, after all. Theory Two is that the tape reduced friction, so the toe strap could be more snug (and less comfortable), especially for the sprint. Kelly was frugal, and he didn't care about pain, so take your pick. Maybe he will tell us someday, and it will be neither theory.

The French ski-binding manufacturer Look was just introducing its step-in binding for Cycling shoes around this time. This system required a specific spring-loaded pedal and a compatible cleat under the shoe. It was a revolution. Frenchman Bernard Hinault led the charge to adopt them, and every sensible professional and civilian began to upgrade. Everyone that is,

---

2 Tightening of toe straps was a 'tell': a sure sign something was about to happen, and you'd better pay attention. Like people messing with their gear selection just that bit too much, this was a giveaway signal of imminent excitement. When professional Cyclists start to eject edible food from their jersey pockets, throw away their amazingly heavy empty bidons or discharge just some of the water from a bidon on to the road before the last climb, something is about to go down.

except for Sean Kelly, *thank you very much, fecking fancy French pedals, not so fast.* He may well have been the last rider in the peloton to switch over, years later.

The guy was old school. If it worked, don't feck with it.

27

MAPEI

Destroying Cobbles, Selling Glue, Forging Rules

Think of legendary sporting teams, and names such as Real Madrid, the New York Yankees and the All Blacks come to mind. The average beer-swilling, hot-dog- or meat-pie-eating fan on the street would be able to reel off most of those names (or their own particular favourite franchise) before you could ask 'Can you even see your toes, dude?' But offer up the name Mapei and – unless they've been doing some floor tiling or vinyl bonding recently – you'll probably be met with an even blanker stare than the one you'd get if you offered them a banana.

But Mapei was a legendary team because it was full of kickass *klassiekers*. For a team's rider to win a major race is a fine achievement which brings prestige and glory for the sponsors and the staff. If the race is a Monument, then the prestige increases tenfold. Not just to win a Monument – the *biggest* Monument – on five occasions but to sweep the podium on three of those five is not just domination; it's bordering on otherworldly invincibility.

Many fans will know of the famous Mapei 1-2-3 at Paris–Roubaix in 1996, when Johan Museeuw was nominated the winner – by Mr Mapei himself, Giorgio Squinzi, founder of that famous floor-laying adhesive empire and principal sponsor of this team – over Gianluca Bortolami and Andrea Tafi. But few

Mambo!

are aware that Mapei repeated the trick, twice, in 1998 and 1999. Those occasions might go relatively unnoticed owing to the fact that the 1996 win was one of those Gewiss-esque moments, with the three teammates time-trialling from 90 km out and arriving together in the velodrome, where they would make a formation that airshow stunt pilots would be envious of as they rolled across the line. The other two occasions weren't as obvious to the naked eye but were no less than demonstrations of a team of superstars making up a superstar team.

Each rider on those Mapei squads of the 1990s could command an entry into this book on his own merit. The aforementioned riders, plus Belgian and Italian studs such as Franco Ballerini, Wilfried Peeters, Tom Steels, Frank Vandenbroucke, Paolo Bettini, Daniele Nardello and Michele Bartoli, place Mapei in the pantheon of a truly stacked Classics squad that was nearly unbeatable, not just on the Flandrian stones but on the *côtes* and *muurs* of the Ardennes as well. There wasn't a Mapei squad that didn't feature near the top of the UCI rankings, winning the prize from 1994 to 2000, and then again in 2002, just before Squinzi pulled the plug on Mapei's ten-year reign of Classics destruction. It wasn't the case in the Grand Tours, though, with Tony Rominger the only real specialist in the longer races who had any support, and even then his Giro and Vuelta wins were more down to his own strength than any support super-*domestiques*. No, Mapei were a true *klassieker* team; they didn't care much for riding stage races – they always preferred a day out on the cobbles.

And they are still around today. Patrick Lefevere – or Patrick The Fever if you prefer, which we do – acquired the team and sought out new sponsors, and the beginnings of what we now know as Etixx–Quick-Step was forged. And the theme of 'Classics powerhouses, GT minnows' carried on until recently, when it began to change with riders like Dan Martin entering the ranks. The backbone of this period in the Lefevere empire was one Tommeke Boonen. He was destined to be a Classics man for the ages when he took third place in his first Pro Paris–Roubaix at the age of twenty-three, with a masterful display of how to ride wet *pavé*. Right then and there – as he watched his US Postal team leader George Hincapie throw himself and his Roubaix ambitions into the Camphin-en-Pévèle ditch – pundits started deploying the 'Next Lion of Flanders' tag with abandon. Museeuw, the existing holder of the 'Lion of Flanders' moniker, saw the writing on the wall and offered to take young Tom under his tutelage, but not before soloing away to his third and last victory in the velodrome.

The Lion Cub was ready to ascend to the Alpha role. Like Sean Kelly and Museeuw before him, Boonen showed off his all-rounder skills and took a green jersey and a bunch of sprint stages at the Tour de France, as well as a World Championship, and then, as his sprinting abilities began to wane, he concentrated on the two races that make a Belgian a *flahute*: the Ronde van Vlaanderen and Paris–Roubaix.[1] Supported by typically stacked Lefevere squads and with Museeuw as his friend and mentor, he won in sprints and he won solo, at both races.

Mapei left an aesthetic as well as sporting legacy. They wore some of the ugliest yet coolest kit in the history of ugly but cool kits. If ever there was a kit that would personify and reinforce Rule #17, it was this: a mix of coloured shapes which may have been intended to represent tiles, jumbled up a bit and stuck on a jersey with super-strength (Mapei) adhesive.[2] It would hurt your eyes to look at, which may be part of the reason they were so good at riding off the front. Mere mortals should not attempt to wear it, but damn if those badasses didn't look the tits powering across the cobbles in it. In fact, the Mapei-GB kit that the '96 Roubaix Inquisition was decked in was relatively understated compared with the optic assaults that followed. So, if anything, we have the greatest Classics squad of all time to thank for bringing the creed of Rule #17 to us in the most Hardman style possible.

---

1 *Flahute* is an untranslatable term, coined by the French, associated with desperately tough Belgian riders.
2 Rule #17 // Team kit is for members of the team. Wearing Pro team kit is also questionable if you're not paid to wear it. If you must fly the colours of Pro teams, all garments should match perfectly: e.g. no Mapei jersey with Kelme shorts and Telekom socks.

ANDREI TCHMIL

Paris–Roubaix 1994

I ride to win, winning is the reason for my existence. That's what I always think at the first races of the season, when I notice the opponents are younger once more. At the first races in the South of France I saw them again: all the new pros who will ride their first pro races. All with high expectations, fresh ambitions, high hopes, shaved legs. Then they see a guy like me: a bit selfish, calm, very experienced, stubborn, self-assured. In a way of speaking I could have been their father. I never wanted to upset their balance, but they should know that it is a new world they are entering. But that is what they know two days later when the first dreams are shattered. I wish them good luck though, but nothing more. Besides, we are opponents, aren't we?

Andrei Tchmil

Sweet Jesus. This guy, where do we start with this fucking guy? He was so hard he made the Flemish Hardmen question their mettle. Tchmil was born in far eastern Russia, deep in the Soviet era. No doubt he was selected for hardness as a youth. In American schools a 'field day' is traditionally held, during which every kid runs a foot race or is lined up for the much-feared 'rope climb'. It's a classic pre-adolescent opportunity to experience public shame, but at least everyone gets a ribbon. We're all winners, aren't we? Not in the USSR. *Their* field days featured stopwatches, clipboards, the KGB and zero ribbons. Anyone who had an aptitude for suffering wound up in a sports school, where training as a professional would begin at a very young age. General hardness was a given – all Soviet kids were tough – but the Stalin Badge for Hardness was only bestowed on the hardest of ten-year-olds. The men with the clipboards collected data on cunning, intimidation, lack of empathy and inability to cry. Vladimir Putin, Alexander Vinokourov,[1] Ivan Drago, Andrei Tchmil. All selected.

With the dissolution of the USSR, some serious Soviet Cycling talent began to flow into the professional peloton. Enter the Alfa Lum team, an Italian team that saw the opportunity to unleash some Soviet hardness – Tchmil included – upon the unsuspecting West, to very good effect. After his time at Alfa Lum, Andrei made the natural migration to Belgium and spent the formative part of his career with the Lotto team. The Italians were a little too soft and fancy for him.

Andrei just naturally rode like a Flandrian. His wins in Milan–Sanremo, the Ronde van Vlaanderen and Paris–Roubaix were all solo finishes. In the Milan–Sanremo he bolted in the last kilometre, holding off the whole sprint-crazed peloton. In the Ronde he went from further out and still held off the bunch. In Paris–Roubaix he casually rode away from a group from way, way out and hammered alone to the velodrome. That Paris–Roubaix win was his first Monument, and had he won nothing else, he would still command much respect at the Hardman's Table. The course had been properly wetted the days prior to that Sunday in April. So much snow and sleet had fallen that week that many feared the race would be cancelled. Except for a cold wind, the start was uneventful. A large lead group entered the

---

1 Unrepentant doper and least popular ever winner of an Olympic bike race.

*Yes, the kit is perfect; pity about the muddy
cobbles Andrei is about to ride over.*

Trouée d'Arenberg with the sun out and everyone's kit clean.
As they emerged the other end, Tchmil rode at the front of the
diminished lead group. He was wise. A crash in the forest had
delayed many of the riders behind him. He had also left his arm
warmers and cotton cap on; maybe he knew something the others
didn't. The sky darkened as the race rolled further north. Once
the rain started up again, the saturated cobbled *secteurs* became

treacherous. The lead group grew in numbers. There were too many past and future winners in it, too many for Andrei. With almost 60 km left, he rolled off the front; no one behind was interested in chasing down a lone rider. And no one was crazy enough to ride away solo in that wind. He slowly built up a marginal gap as big hitters behind refused to be the ones burning their matches to chase.[2] Then the punctures started on the slippery cobbles, and the team cars were unable to get through to their riders. Except Tchmil's, because the gap he had opened up on the chasing group was now large enough for the commissar to allow the Lotto support car forward. Now Andrei had spare wheels, a spare bike, food and drinks, all for the asking. A puncture for him might cost thirty seconds; a puncture for a team leader in the group behind could mean Race Over.

The slick cobbled *secteurs* came one after another. Johan Museeuw, Tchmil's ex-teammate, slowly closed in, only ten seconds behind. Rather than sit up and wait so the two could work together toward the velodrome, Tchmil kept grinding it out. Museeuw was on an experimental full suspension rig but he was *not* floating over the cobbles. The minuscule gap held for ages; the catch seemed inevitable; then Museeuw cracked. The gap went up again to thirty-five seconds. Tchmil was flying.

The TV motorbike paused as Museeuw stopped and his team car pulled up. Johan was switching bikes, but he couldn't get his feet out of his grit-fouled pedals. There was much Flemish swearing that day, friends. Somehow the mechanic kept him balanced and wrenched his right foot out from the pedal. The

---

2 A Cycling expression for energy allotment. At the beginning of each race you start with a full box of matches. Every time you chase someone down, or chase back from a puncture or put your face into the wind you burn a match and you can't get another from the team car. How well you save and use your matches determines your result. Cycling analogies for fatigue are endless: running on fumes, smoking like a hippie's motorbike, cracked, *jour sans*.

suspension bike was literally ditched; time was lost. Museeuw was back on a real bike, and Tchmil was still hammering on to victory in the velodrome. Tchmil must have cracked Museeuw badly; the 'Lion of Flanders' came in over four minutes down, in thirteenth place. Out of 191 starters there were forty-eight finishers. Fabio Baldato, in second place, crashed three times and had five punctures. *That* was second place?

Andrei Tchmil crossed the glossy wet finish line in the velodrome with a huge satisfied smile. No helmet – he had pitched his white cotton cap as it was slowing him down somehow – no eyewear and no mud on his shoulders or hips; no crashes.

How does a Hardman, or an aspirant Hardman avoid second place? You ride at the front so you can pick your line across the manure-covered cobbles, with fewer crashes and fewer punctures. You ride the crown; it's smoother and it's faster.[3] When a Flandrian is closing in on you, you go deeper, you hold him back there, and you keep dishing it out until you crush his little Flemish will.

---

3 The cobbled *secteurs* of Paris–Roubaix often have a pronounced crown across the path. Centuries of ox carts and farm machinery have formed it. It's not necessarily smoother, but it is drier, with no puddles and fewer surprises. Riding the crown is how it's done; you can see what's ahead. It may take a bit more work, but your future course can be seen even if that future is only the next ten metres ahead. Obviously this is also a manure-covered metaphor for getting through life.

PETER VAN PETEGEM

April 2001

Peter van Petegem's two wins in the Ronde van Vlaanderen and his victory in the 2003 Paris–Roubaix made him a proper Flandrian *klassieker*, the Cycling equivalent of a Mafia 'made man'. Like our Sicilian friends, van Petegem also sports a five o'clock shadow at 7 a.m., as he leaves the bath from his morning shave. We can never hear enough stories told from inside the race. But there is one moment that explains a lot about Peter van Petegem.

In 2001 Peter was hired by the doomed American Mercury-Viatel team, hoping to bring their American success to the Continent. Buying success is never a sure thing, but hiring van Petegem seemed as close as they could get. Ultimately, the project would fail as Viatel went bust and the operation went into the ditch. But in April 2001 they were still active and facing a classically nasty Paris–Roubaix.

> So, before the race, we were huddled up in the team camper van. I'd like to say team bus, but it really wasn't. The weather was so bad the bus was rocking from side to side from the wind, and we could hardly hear each other speak because the rain drumming on the roof was so loud. Greg LeMond came in to see us, as we were riding

Many of the weaker riders have already been defeated!

his bikes that year. He'd just given an interview with some TV guys, and was soaked through. He looked like someone had turned a fire hose on him. He could hardly look us in the eye as he wished us good luck for the race. Then in came Peter van Petegem, our team leader for our classics campaign that year. He was beaming this huge smile as he looked around the van, his eyes sparkling and his whole being literally glowing. 'I like this weather!' he proclaimed. 'It is good for us. Many of the weaker riders have already been defeated.' Suddenly the prospect of going out there and racing didn't seem so bad.

Sadly, 2001 was not to be our year: PVP got caught behind one too many crashes, and missed the decisive break – line honours that year went to Servais Knaven, and PVP only managed 24th. It was not until 2003 that he won Paris–Roubaix, but his words that day confirmed to me that he was a true legend of our sport.

Derek Bouchard-Hall, Mercury–Viatel teammate

Indeed, 2001 was one of the last properly wet, horrible Paris–Roubaix races. Servais Knaven soloed in triumphant but unrecognisable even to his mother, completely coated in that fine northern French road paste. To thrive in those conditions means one has grown up training and racing in them. The unrelenting wind blowing off the cold North Sea makes the average day on the bike tough. When you grow up accepting that as normal, you are a different kind of Cyclist.

Every Pro would like to ride cobbles in terrible weather like Peter van Petegem. Very few actually can. We civilians can hope to manage it in very brief intervals, if at all. If one comes into a section of *pavé* with the correct amount of pace (high, but not out of control) in the correct gear (big chainring but turning it over well), one can feel like van Petegem for just a little while … and we're talking *seconds* here.

Do you want to ride like PVP? OK, that's not going to happen, but if you want at least to *look* like you ride like PVP: develop massive guns and imperviousness to conditions by growing up in Flanders and racing up its steep cobbled *bergs* on a daily basis, acquire a steely yet unaffected gaze even when suffering mightily while dropping fellow Belgians, lose 12 kilos no matter what you weigh and don't shave for three days.

PART IV
LES DOMESTIQUES

'I get paid to hurt people. How good is that?'

Jens Voigt, Hardman

Some of us crave personal success; some find satisfaction in the service of others. *Domestiques* are the riders who work to support other members of their team; they sit on the front of the bunch for hours on end, relentlessly churning a beat on the pedals, for little or no personal glory. A hard day's work, a job well done, the knowledge that their efforts helped the team in some way: for the *domestique* these things are their own reward. They are self-evident and require no external affirmation.

Domestiques have the capacity to suffer in ways that other racers aren't required to. They are the ones who are sent to the front of the group to close the gap to a dangerous breakaway or to ferry their team leader back to the peloton after a puncture, crash, mechanical problem or sudden and undiagnosable physiological problem often accompanied by loads of insufferable whining. Is the team leader feeling a bit parched or getting a spot peckish? The *domestique* goes back to the team car, loads his jersey pockets with food and water and rides back up to deliver the goods to their captain. Is the weather getting a bit dodgy and they fancy themselves to be riding in a rain cape? Back to the team car with you. Oh, now that the rain cape has become a bore because the weather got peachy again? *Be a sport and carry it back to the car, would you?*

There are different breeds of *domestiques*. Some are big, burly riders who push a hole through the wind like a sheet of plywood. They are handy for the team on long, flat stages or during windy stretches along the North Sea in the Spring Classics. Others are lightweight climbers who set the pace for the team leader in the mountains; they churn out a relentless tempo to discourage rivals from attacking, setting the stage for their team captain to put them all to the sword. Finally, there are *domestiques* who make up a sprinter's lead-out train: fast, powerful riders who notch up the speed of the entire bunch bit by bit over the final kilometres while their leader sits in, waiting for the perfect moment to launch his own sprint and get to the line first.

Mario Cipollini was the most dominant sprinter in the 1990s and 2000s, largely thanks to his *domestiques*. His lead-out train would ride so fast that, by the time he burned through them all, all he had to do was maintain the speed of his last *domestique* in order to win the sprint; rare was the occasion that a rider had the power to emerge from his slipstream and come around him. On the other hand, Mark Cavendish tends to sprint from much less organised trains, and instead relies on a smaller set of ultra-specialised lead-out men like Mark Renshaw. To hear Cav talk of Renshaw's qualities makes you feel they are closer than brothers, tuned into one another as if through some kind of symbiotic neural connection. Who knows, maybe they are avatars? In any case, Cav relies heavily on Renshaw to guide him through the bunch, positioning him perfectly to launch his sprint. The Velominati have even gone so far as to rename him Mark Rickshaw or simply FedEx. (He always delivers his package on time.)

Lance Armstrong 'won' each of his seven Tours de France on the backs of his small legion of workers: George Hincapie was the sheet of plywood he sat behind on the flats; Tyler Hamilton, Roberto Heras and Floyd Landis paced him up the mountain passes, setting a tempo so high no one dared dream of attacking. Not including time trials, he probably spent less than 25 km of any Tour riding on the front. That works out to be roughly 1 per cent of the race.

Make no mistake: *domestiques* (or *gregarios* if on an Italian team) are hugely talented Cyclists; indeed many are national champions. They can be race winners when their leader has bad legs or if they are in a breakaway group that unexpectedly isn't caught. Eddy Merckx would sometimes (but rarely) spread around the wealth by letting one of his men attack off the front when the win looked ripe for the picking. Eddy would then drive his *directeur sportif* crazy by asking for status updates every ten minutes. Is he strong? Is he going well enough? If the *directeur sportif* was *at all* doubtful, Eddy would attack to win himself.

Eddy paid the best riders to race *for* him, rather than race *against* him on another team. Not unlike Chris Froome's Tour de France Sky squad, in which every man could be the leader of another team. Curiously, those talented riders who serve and then eventually step out from under the shadow of a dominant leader to seek their own glory usually come up short of their new ambitions. Some, such as Floyd Landis, take the opportunity straight away and deliver by winning big (even if that win will be tainted for ever), while many more, like Tyler Hamilton, don't benefit from the right combination of luck, form, pharmacology and favourable opponents to ever grasp that last rung on the ladder. Maybe some don't really want to desert their regimen of duty and are most comfortable serving their leader and sharing in the spoils that way. Maybe their humility, versatility and loyalty are paradoxically the best weapons in their arsenal and the ones they know how to use to best effect. To win consistently as a leader requires a killer instinct, a transformation into another personality that emerges only during fierce competition. Not everyone has that edge, that ability to take risks in order to win at all costs. *Domestiques* know themselves well and understand there is more than one way to be exceptional at racing bikes.

TONY MARTIN

'Panzerwagen'

Kids don't polish their bikes to a high gloss while dreaming of being a *domestique*. As those kids start to crush fools first locally, regionally, then nationally, they see themselves as future leaders of professional teams, crushing *all* fools. Of course, their first season at the professional level is a great reality check. All these riders are stronger, faster and tougher than I am? I didn't sign up for this, grovelling at the back all day.

Life at the top of the pyramid is rough as well. Every Pro has a huge capacity to endure. Each has his or her strengths, and not every race is suited to them, so every Pro gets to carry water bottles at some point. Bernard Hinault must have done it, for one race at least, as a first-year professional on the Gitane–Campagnolo team. But he would not have been happy about it. Here is your fucking bidon, Monsieur Van Impe. Don't get used to this.

Most modern riders have to shoulder some *domestique* work at some point in their career. Even multiple time trial world champion Tony Martin has done his fair share. He is no sprinter or *grimpeur*, but he is a proper teammate. If the day's stage is heading for a sprint finish, you'll see Tony Martin more than once with a jersey full of bidons, working his way up through the team cars and back to the peloton, to pass them out to his colleagues. Later you'll see him putting his giant motor to good use chasing down the break. And finally he is there in the lead-out train, mouth agape, hauling serious ass, finishing up all his *domestique* duties. In 2016's Paris–Roubaix, Tony made quite the début on the stones by personally taking it upon himself to tow Tom Boonen across *secteur* after *secteur,* splitting the race and leaving carnage in his wake. Not bad for a first-timer on the hallowed ground.

Yes, he loves the big ring and may be the only professional who regularly puts a 58-tooth chainring on his time trial bike and survives. He wears the armbands of World Champion (three times!) in the time trial. So when he is in a two-up breakaway in the Vosges mountains in the Tour de France, as he was on Day Nine of the 2014 Tour, everyone starts talking. And most of the talk is: he won't survive; he is no climber; he only knows the big ring. Talk is cheap to Tony. His mouth may be agape, but it's his legs that are making all the noise. A large group had got away after the start, and from that group Italian Alessandro De Marchi broke free, followed quickly by Martin. One would think having a strong breakaway companion – even if not a lightweight climber – would be welcome on a stage with six categorised climbs. Perhaps Alessandro did think that that, but only for a while.

After which, what he thought was, this guy is killing me. When Tony was on the front, he was going so strongly up each climb that Alessandro was getting zero rest behind, working way harder than he should have been just to stay on his companion's wheel. Then De Marchi had to go to the front and work some more. It was painful to watch. And then Martin dropped him.

I think there are not so many guys in Cycling who can do it like this, but I have to do it this way because I am not a guy for the big attacks and playing games. When I have the space, when I have a

Der Panzerwagen. Even says so on the cap.

gap, I know I can make a good race and go really fast. I can do an effort like that in more than a one-hour time trial. I can put out this kind of effort in a three- or four-hour mountain stage … So, it was all or nothing. Uphill most of the time everybody goes fast, but on the descents and the flats you can really make up time. Because everybody in the big break is too busy watching each other. That happened behind us. Uphill we maybe did the same speed, but on the top of the climbs and the descents we made really good time.

Tony Martin

Tony worked each climb that day like he would a time trial: go to the edge of blowing up and stay there; descend like a demon; repeat. Tony is letting us all in on something important here. Go hard over the crest of a hill, to set up your descent just as most riders are switching off their effort. There is much to be gained by this little move. If you are not a climber and better on the flats, use it. Don't lose too much on the climbs then work your way back, both descending and on the flatter sections in between.

Having put Alessandro out of his misery on the last climb of the day – the Markstein – Der Panzerwagen won the stage and pulled on the dotty jumper. Not bad for a part-time world champion time trialist and full-time *domestique*.[1]

---

1 *Panzerwagen* is German for 'armoured car'. Think of German Tony Martin as an armoured-up, unstoppable, uncrushable, impenetrable, rolling heavy, absolutely badass, punishing machine. And yes, this 'Panzerwagen' name started politically correct fires in the comment sections of a few Cycling sites. The Velominati site was not one of them: we all seemed oddly comfortable with the idea of a German rider crushing everyone on French soil being called Panzerwagen. What else could you call him?

MATHEW HAYMAN

Paris–Roubaix 2016 – Journey(man) to Hell

Journeyman. It's not the most flattering description for a Pro Cyclist, implying, as it does, a rider who's been around a few teams, never really being given the chance to do something for themselves, always in the service of others. Sometimes, though, these riders, valuable yet unsung, find themselves in just the right break, in the right race, on the right day, and take full advantage of the situation.

Johan Vansummeren was one such beneficiary of circumstance at Paris–Roubaix in 2010, and took the crowning prize to cap a career spent in toil. Such a win, when the favourites cancel each other out or suffer the bad luck that befalls many on the race's infamous cobblestones, is always warmly received, with no loyalties to the big names clouding anyone's emotions, where the underdog wins one for all of us. JVS didn't have to do anything on the bike again, his Belgian hero status ensuring he couldn't enter so much as a urinal without heads turning. If you're only going to win one big race in your career, you might as well make it a Monument.

When you're thirty-seven and coming back from a broken arm, simply getting into an early breakaway group in your favourite race seems like a foolproof plan: a bit of telly time for you and your sponsor, don't work *too* much, be there for your leader when he arrives and you have to wring yourself dry of whatever juice you've got left in the tank and then pop off the back for the crawl home.

Either that or you can win the race.

Matty Hayman. His very name says 'average bloke'. He could be a plumber or a farmer or a milkman or that nice bloke down the pub who no one knows exactly what he does. Cyclists who win big races have fancy names, like Fabian, Chris or ... Tom. Actually, never mind. Still, Matty fucking Hayman was never supposed to win big bike races, mate. Not with a name like that. And he sure as hell wasn't supposed to be the one to deny the biggest name in cobbled racing his fifth (record-breaking) Paris–Roubaix. Matty missed the memo on that one. He found himself at the business end of his favourite race and decided to give it a red-hot go.

It's rare for the day's early break to result in much other than a few 'heroic rides' at any race, let alone Paris–Roubaix, when a lone rider might ultimately hang on for a top ten or top twenty placing at the finish (albeit a fine result for most who take on the 265 km trip through Hell). Hayman had tasted the top ten a couple of times before, and on this occasion he wasn't really thinking beyond working for his team leader, Jens Keukeleire, and getting himself to the finish on the Roubaix velodrome in one piece. Particularly since he had broken his arm only six weeks earlier. But this time the breakaway, or the remnants of it, stayed away and Hayman beat them all to the line.

These Pros? They are Not Normal. They have something wired differently, or their pain receptors removed, or they're not smart enough to wonder why going so batshit hard hurts, or something. And Pros who contest Paris–Roubaix time after time and even profess to love the race are even more Not Normal. This love is what drives a Hardman to return fifteen times, plugging away in dutiful service, until everything suddenly and spectacularly falls

Y-M-C-A!

into place. And on that day you fear no one, respect everyone and race like you're the biggest rider on the road. And on that day you win one for the journeymen. Legend cemented.

JENS VOIGT

Conan's Great Battle

At one point Conan [the Barbarian] and his other old warrior friends capture this village, but then they find that they are surrounded by an army of tens of thousands, and his only reaction is, 'Oh man, it's going to take days to kill all these people!'

Jens Voigt, post-race interview

The Velominati have a theory that in order to be a great athlete one needs to display the 'Perfect Amount of Dumb'. Professional athletes – and Cyclists in particular – are an impressive bunch. They are tough, disciplined people who ply their trade in some of the most atrocious conditions imaginable. To become Pros they have to be good at what they do and smart enough to learn how to continue succeeding despite the ever-narrowing gaps in quality between athletes as they continue their rise to the top. They have to learn to live right and train right. They have to listen to their coaches when their bodies are telling them something else. They have to learn to control their mind and to overrule their lungs and legs. They need to be smart enough to read an ever-changing race and recognise the moment to make their move; disaster and glory can be separated only by a

split-second reaction born out of intuition mixed with experience and intelligence.

But the best athletes are also a little bit dumb. These are the
men and women who flog themselves for hours on end and,
when their bodies are about to break, dial it up another notch. A
smarter athlete might consider the possibility of slowing down
or not going at all. This characteristic flows as a strong current in
the Sea of *Domestiques*; riding on the front with the sole purpose
of making everyone behind you suffer is not the work for the
intelligentsia, and Merckx bless them for it. These are riders who
find some sinister pleasure in knowing they made the race hard,
even if they cross the finish line hours after the winner, with a
twisted grin on their face.

No one embodies the Perfect Amount of Dumb better than
Jens Voigt, who truly loved his work and may even be the happiest person on the planet, judging by the insane positivity of his
interviews. One of his most famous quotes was prior to the 2012
Tour de France, when being interviewed by NBC Sports. He was
describing the internal dialogue that occurs when he is sitting
on the front or in a breakaway:

> Ah, it hurts so bad and then you say, 'Shut up legs, do what I tell you
> to do!' And then sometimes it works! And then you GO!

His post-race, hypoxic interviews were even more entertaining:
with his mind further incapacitated by oxygen debt from four
hours spent deep within the Pain Cave, his stories were as mysterious and funny as those of a giddy toddler explaining the plot
of *Star Wars*.[1]

---

1 The Pain Cave is the dark and lonely place we go in our minds when
suffering like spanked goats. The Pain Cave is made up of a series of caverns,
each deeper and darker than the next. As we learn to suffer, we uncover the
secret path that takes us further and deeper within. Sounds like fun, no?

Giving it the berries, leg slime free of charge.

Jens was an unusual kind of *domestique*. He didn't fit into the 'service-only' mould; he was happiest having people suffer on his wheel, but he won his fair share of races by being in the right break at the right time, and having the instinct to take full advantage of the bird in hand, so to speak. He won a gigantic diamond by winning a stage of the Tour de France; he won Paris–Nice as well as the Tour of Germany by being a hard nutter with too little brains to wonder whether he should stop pushing on the pedals. Ever.

Here is Jens looking like a Whale Shark, doing his best to break either his bike or the tarmac, whichever comes first. He's in the leader's jersey of Paris–Nice, and he has his own slime on his shorts. We won't speculate on whether said slime is ocular, nasal or oral, but by the looks of his expression it is probably all three. (Ocular slime is like a tear, but thicker. It only happens when you want to cry from pain, but there isn't any water left in the system for actual 'tears'. Science. Look it up.) If memory serves, he lost that Paris–Nice, giving it the berries. But maybe he won. It doesn't matter because he was giving it the berries and sometimes giving it the berries feels almost as good as winning.

Jens did have a propensity to fall off his bike when going fast. It was normal for him. On one occasion he came off (on camera) more than three times on one descent, after which he actually shrugged at the moto camera stopping to film him as if to say, 'I know, rubber side down, rubber side down. But rubber side keeps going up. So I just keep going as much as I can while the rubber side is still down. Yes?'

His most famous *chute* was in the Tour of 2010, when he managed to arrange an impromptu high-speed yard sale. His bike surprised him by being in two pieces when he went to collect it. One bike, twice the money! That's a solid return on investment, assuming you don't need to keep riding the bike, which he did. So he did what any sensible person would do: borrowed a junior's bike from a nearby spectator and rode off down the mountain on it. He eventually received a spare team bike that fit and he finished the stage within the time limit. That's Rule #5. We should all be more like Jens.

ADAM HANSEN

Batman

Sixteen Grand Tours and counting, Adam Hansen can do it all. Want him in the break? He can do that. Want him to actually win the stage from that break? Done. Want him to design and fabricate his own ultra-lightweight carbon Cycling shoes? Too late, he did that on his own.

This may seem obvious, but it is worth saying: if you are riding for a living, you have to love riding your bike. A professional spends an unholy number of hours on the bike each year, and most of it is training. You train to race. And yet, as with many other Cycling conventions, Adam Hansen has rethought that one. He races to race. His high-altitude training camp for the Tour de France was the Giro d'Italia. His Vuelta a España preparation was the Tour de France. Normally that's not done, because normal humans can't do that. A normal human would do one Grand Tour a year, or maybe the Giro and then the Vuelta, with a large recovery between. And that would be quite enough, thank you.

What makes Hansen a Hardman is riding sixteen *consecutive* Grand Tours (up to and including the 2016 Vuelta) and finishing them all. Ride the Giro, recover, ride the Tour, recover, ride the Vuelta, year after year after year. It's hard enough to even be *selected* for one Grand Tour as a rider, much less sixteen consecutive ones. That is an incredible feat in itself, but Adam works each stage: he leads out André 'The Gorilla' Greipel, gets in breaks, chases down breaks, wins stages and carries bottles. He also enjoyed a handed-up beer during the Tour stage where L'Alpe d'Huez was climbed twice. This is a rider to love. When most other riders are cursing the organisers of the stage, Adam sees the crazy and manages to enjoy it. Every Grand Tour rider gets sick and gets tangled up in crashes. Adam does too, but he soldiers on, recovers and somehow shows up for the next one.

That many racing days give a rider time to ponder his predicament. Adam is an engineer by training, so he knows weight and drag are key numbers to minimise. Reducing everyday drag for a professional Cyclist means modifying one's position. Frames and wheels have already been made more aero in the wind tunnels, so the biggest gains available come from improving the aerodynamics of the rider. If there are marginal gains to be had, he will have them.[1] Adam decided to maximise his drop and start using narrow bars.[2] Maximising his drop meant his riding position got lower and flatter. As for the narrow bars, well, back in the 1980s the thinking was that handlebars should be as wide as your shoulders, 'to keep your chest open'. Adam, the engineer, questioned this and realised that bringing your arms in was more aero, open chest or no. So he started to use narrower bars. Simple.

---

1 Marginal gains is Team Sky Principal Sir David Brailsford's concept of many very small improvements, combining to bring success. Millions of British pounds later, Sir Dave could have saved most of it by just following Adam Hansen around for a few days, collecting free ideas.
2 'The drop' is the vertical distance between saddle and handlebars. Like 'showing post', this is something the civilian maximises in order to look more Pro. As with the showing of post, it has resulted in a lot of people with handlebars so low they can't physically ride in the drops. Which is what is known as a Sub Optimal Outcome.

That is about as simple as it gets.

Our Adam makes his own minimalist Cycling shoes out of carbon fibre, and wears a skinsuit *always*; he is like Batman, if Batman fired his manservant and made all his own high-tech bling. Besides the bike and wheels, Cycling shoes are the most expensive, highly engineered, hotly debated item a Cyclist will own. The quickest way to start a slap-fight with a Cyclist is to query their footwear. But Adam has his own ideas; these things on my feet should be lighter. Let's see: 40 grams less per pedal stroke, times the number of pedal strokes per year ... that can't be right, 155 metric fucktons? I'd better get on that. So he eventually starts making shoes he can race in, Grand Tour after Grand

Tour. They are unique. The fit, the cleat position, the single tight-ening knob, all very Adam Hansen.

Ten years ago he was already re-sewing his jerseys to make them fit more snugly. And ten years ago he was the only person thinking about that. His Highroad teammates back then must have wondered why he was making the effort. That's just a mar-ginal gain. Right along with crashes and respiratory infections, the much-dreaded saddle sore is a hazard to avoid if one wishes to continue in stage races. The care and grooming of Adam's groin must surpass the David Zabriskie level of fanaticism.[3] Either that or he just has the iron ass of a Hardman. We don't really want to know.

He gets away from the bike for long stretches: climbs to Everest base camp, competes in ultra-marathons, generally runs around the world staying active. He stays off the bike for huge intervals, doing other aerobic activities. This is an important lesson, this time away from two wheels. Many of us have been slaves to the saddle, feeling we must put in the kilometres every week, year after year. It will lead to burnout and bodily harm. To avoid burnout and the Belleville effect, try being decent (not totally sucking) at another aerobic sport or two, one that uses arms and upper body occasionally.[4] Not golf, obviously. But if you *have* to play golf, keep your mouth shut about it to other Cyclists. We don't care.

And yes, most of us have already sucked at all other sports, hence becoming Cyclists. To be a Cyclist requires nothing more

---

3 Ex-Pro Cyclist David Zabriskie really took care of his butt. He started his own chamois crème business, DZNUTS, and has published his own fastidious hygienic methodology for avoiding saddle sores. It involves the daily use of shaving cream, razors, antiseptics, ultraviolet lights for sterilisation purposes and, of course, lots of chamois crème lube.
4 The Belleville effect: from the film *Belleville Rendez-vous* (*The Triplets of Belleville* in the US), a must-watch animated Cycling film where all the riders have massive legs but twiggy upper bodies.

than staying upright on a bike and trying hard. There are no hand-eye coordination aptitudes in Cycling. A good follow-through, balance, timing, technique … none of these things is actually requisite. Just ride the bike. A four-year-old can do it, for fuck's sake. Like anything, getting good at it requires major commitment. But really, practically *only* commitment. No membership fees, no lessons, just flying down the road, just like that four-year-old.

The C-word (commitment) is a loaded word for Cyclists. It's mainly a positive thing, this self-requirement to spend loads of time on the bike, often alone, in all kinds of weather. But it will take a toll on relationships, maybe career, certainly all other interests. Yet despite those potential landmines, that same commitment will keep a person from getting fat and becoming an alcoholic (because getting up early on Sunday morning for a ride and being hungover are incompatible, over the long run). Concussion? Knocked-out teeth? Ruined knees? Torn shoulders? Nah, none of that, this is a sport for a lifetime.

EROS POLI

Mont Ventoux, Tour de France 1994

The Giant of Provence: Eros Poli.

Have we really defined Hardman yet? It may not be possible. But we have surely established that out-lasting, out-persevering, going further into the Pain Cave and then staying there longer than everyone else are all part of the story.

Eros Poli rode as a *gregario* for Mario Cipollini on the Mercatone Uno–Medeghini Team. Eros was an Olympic Gold Medal holder in the team time trial, an event that should give one automatic Hardman status in itself. The Olympic Team Time Trial was a four-man, 100 km event. The finishing time was taken from the third rider to cross the line. If that third rider was 2 km back, shattered, well, that was not much of a *team* time trial, was it? Consider it. A 100 km paceline at full gas with the front rider on the rivet just long enough for him or her to regain the third person's wheel when they pull off. Pull for too long at the front and you will not regain that sacred draft – you will be off the back. Do the others wait? Do the others even know? They won't know unless you yell you've been dropped, which will only result in a time-wasting regroup. So four riders are riding on the razor's edge of blowing up and going as fast as they can for 100 km. That is a Hardman's event, end of story.

Poli already had his gold medal certification in Hardman riding when he was selected for the 1994 Tour de France. He was one of the diesel engines in the original sprint train, pulling Mario Cipollini to the line. Eros is almost 2 metres tall, built for speed and power on the flat finishing kilometres of a sprint. Super Mario was not present (rumoured hair perm catastrophe) when the 1994 Tour de France started, so Eros had a little more scope to race for himself. What was the plan on Stage 15 for the Italian Mercatone Uno–Medeghini team – a sprinters' team without a sprinter – when that day's race menu looked so unpalatable? Between the start in Montpellier and the finish in Carpentras stood the Giant of Provence, Mont Ventoux. For most non-climbers the main objective would be not to miss the time cut.[1] This was

---

1 One of stage racing's harshest rules is the time limit for finishing each day's route, even in time trials. It is varied slightly according to the severity of the stage, but at best it's 15 to 20 per cent longer than the winner's time. Failure to finish within the time limit means pack your bags and go home, no whining. So when some freak of nature like Pantani goes apeshit uphill, everyone at the back of the race has to get very busy not being eliminated. Cycling is cruel.

a climber's stage, so for the non-climber it was a day not to have bad legs and get eliminated. This was a day for that little *elefantino* Marco Pantani from the Carrera Jeans squad. Did Eros put his hand up at the pre-race meeting and say the Italian equivalent of 'Chill the fuck out, guys – I've got this'? We may never know.

It was a boiling hot day in Provence. The pack was cruising; the peloton was tapping out tempo until the real race began on Mont Ventoux. Poli rode off the front a mere 60 km into the stage. One can imagine the shaking of heads among the Pros: Mercatone–Uno needs a little TV time. Oooooof, Eros, we will see you again soon enough. The magnificent Miguel Indurain was in the *maillot jaune*; his job description for the day was just to keep his rivals close. Pantani was already ten minutes down in the overall classification; he would have some freedom for a stage win. Poli had another idea. He had generated a twenty-five-minute lead at the foot of Ventoux. Twenty-five minutes, dear readers! That is an astounding feat. And that was the easy part. He then punished himself and his bike on the slopes of the Giant. He was the opposite of a climber; he was not spinning a short climber's gear; he was not repeatedly jumping out of the saddle; there was no dancing on the pedals. He *was* suffering as only non-climbers have to suffer on unrelenting steep slopes. *Grinta* is what the Italians would say; he showed a lot of *grinta* that day.

The TV announcers were convinced that Pantani, who had eventually dropped all climbing rivals, was on the way to victory. Marco was steadily eating into Eros's time buffer, but by the time Eros struggled over the summit ramp, Marco was still minutes behind. The finish line was still a long, fast, descent and flat approach into Carpentras away. Barring a cataclysmic crash, Poli had already won the stage, but the TV announcers just couldn't get their minds around a *domestique* the size of Poli getting the better of the climbers. You wee climbers can hurt us on the climbs, but we get our revenge on the descent. Climbers simply don't have the mass to bomb a descent like a big *rouleur*.

Big man Eros Poli with his convertible casquette.

Poli flew down the Ventoux and just kept the chain in the 53 × 11 all the way to Carpentras.[2] The tears were flowing by the time he hit the *flamme rouge*. He rode no-hands towards the line, threw his convertible *casquette* into the crowd and took a bow. That's right, he took a bow from the saddle.[3]

---

2 53 × 11 represents his gear ratios. It may or may not be helpful to think of the front chainrings and the rear cogs as the mullet of the bicycle: business in the front, party in the back. While the rear has been partying up a storm over the years, adding cogs and teeth, the front is still all business. Two gears only, the big dog is always a 52 or 53. Triple chainrings shall not be discussed, ever. The smaller/inner front chainring has been beaten down from a 42 to a 39. The 53 × 39 is called the Belgian Compact, as all Belgians normally ride a 53 × 42 or even a 44. In comparison, an actual compact is a very unprofessional and very sissy 50 × 34 gearing.
3 The convertible *casquette* is a cap for hot days, when some shade for the face would be nice. It involves cutting the dome off a cotton cap, leaving

To this day we don't know whether this ride was a team tactic or just a mad plan dreamed up by Eros Poli himself. Certainly no one else tried anything else like it that day. He didn't ask for help. He just did it. For the gravitationally challenged Cyclist, he is a shining beacon of *grinta*, of heart, of strength, of gravel in the gut. Take your chances even when they look bad, and if it all works out, or even if not, take a bow at the end.

---

the wee bill for shade but an open top for heat loss. Poli may or may not have invented this stunning fashion statement. Even if not, he wore it so well he made it his own.

PART V
I VELOCISTI

I'm fascinated by the sprinters. They suffer so much during the race just to get to the finish, they hang on for dear life in the climbs, but then in the final kilometres they are transformed and do amazing things. It's not their force *per se* that impresses me, but rather the renaissance they experience. Seeing them suffer throughout the race only to be reborn in the final is something for fascination.

Miguel Indurain, quoted in Edmund R. Burke, *Serious Cycling*

There's not much to the town line sprint, that staple of club rides all over the world: you make sure no one else in the group is paying attention, then you jump those losers, gleefully giggling as you coast over the line, your 'rivals' behind you, struggling with the massive gear they were in when you made your move. If you ride in a good group that knows the area, the pickings tend to be a little slimmer; an adept rider will be paying attention from a few clicks out and will start to position themselves for the sprint. One rider goes, and everyone jumps after them. If the first rider had any brains at all, they were just messing with everyone and now everyone else is sprinting like crazy from way too far out, the first rider sitting up and watching those fools kick each other's heads in.

If you win a lot of town line sprints, you may have managed to convince yourself that you are good at sprinting. But there is a big difference between what a Pro sprinter does and what even the highest-level amateur rider can manage. First of all, the races are longer. Much longer. And the speeds are higher. Much higher. Which means everyone is already totally fucked by the time it comes time to sprint. Pouncing on a finish line when you're fresh is an entirely different affair from doing it when the tank is empty and the guns were fried a few hours ago.

A flat Grand Tour stage shows us what is required of a world-class sprinter, what it takes even to contest the sprint in the first place, let alone win it. In most cases, the last 10 km of a stage are ridden with the throttle wide open, rider after rider peeling off the front of the race, their job as lead-out monkey performed. The used-up monkey,

A bit of argy-bargy, I think they call it.

done with their job, falls through the bunch like a rock dropped into a pond, the bunch swaying and flowing around them. After all the team's riders are used up, their energies given completely to generating the highest possible speed for the race, there is only one rider left who has a job left to do: *il velocista*, *le sprinteur*, the sprinter.

Imagine the searing pain of racing 200 or more kilometres in a day, *then* following your team mates as they accelerate to 60 kph or more, burning through the lead-out train like stages of a rocket and being left to the last 200 metres to light your own afterburners and get to the finish line first. Did we mention that all along you're fighting for position, bumping elbows, shoulders and unmentionables with riders on every side of you? Did we mention that a moment's inattention means you've lost ten or more places in the line and your victory hopes are dashed? Did we mention that, if you lose your nerve and touch your brakes even for an instant, you might as well forget being a sprinter? Did we mention that this might be the most thrilling and difficult way to win a bike race?

The sprinter has a difficult lot in life. They are a one-trick pony, with an absolutely stunningly impressive trick: they can go bat-shit fast when everyone else can hardly go at all.

But not every day. Introduce a big enough hill into a day's *parcours* and you can forget about them. Which is why a three-week-long Grand Tour is both a sprinter's finest showcase and their agonising nemesis. A Grand Tour contains many hills – mountains, indeed – and has a time limit on every stage, calculated as a percentage of the stage winner's time. Bulky sprinters can never take it easy; they are condemned to suffer through two weeks of climbing, struggling to get their overdeveloped thighs to the finish line within the limit just to contest a handful of flat stages.

A sprinter who can finish a Grand Tour is a Hardman.

FREDDY MAERTENS

Champagne in the Bidon

When I tried once to follow Freddy on his 56 × 12 my legs ached for a week.

Sean Kelly, in Robin Magowan, *Kings of the Road*

Oh Freddy, if the Velominati were at all literate, we would know which Shakespearean tragic hero to compare you to. Like Jan Raas, you had the hardness to get to the finish of any wet, windy Belgian race in the front group. And you had the sprint of an angel, if angels were competitive bastards and God was handing out the legs. And you loved the high life that went along with winning: the champagne, the women, the partying, the tax-evading. All the things that must have made the ascetic Sean Kelly, your understudy, scratch his head and wonder what was actually required of a man to become the dominant sprinter of his day.

Being a Flandrian sprinter means getting over all the *bergs* and surviving the crosswinds just to get to the business end of the race at the front. Freddy could do that. It is said the young Maertens would set out from West Flanders with a tailwind and ride as long and as hard as he could until flat fucked, *then* ride home. Into the wind. The Flemish wind. Which is the worst kind of wind in the world.

Maertens turned Pro under Briek Schotte, *directeur* of the Flandria team and the perfect, no-nonsense taskmaster.[1] At this time Merckx was still King Eddy of Belgium, and young Maertens didn't care much for that. In those days the Belgian Cycling royalty – Merckx, Godefroot, De Vlaeminck – were treated with great deference. They split the wins between them while the young Pros were happy to fight for the scraps. But young Freddy found he could outsprint Eddy. And so he did.

They clashed at the World Championships, both riding for Belgium. Towards the finish Eddy, Freddy, Felice Gimondi and Luis Ocaña were away from the following group. The young Maertens offered to lead out Merckx. Merckx told him to kick early; Freddy did; Merckx didn't have the legs to follow him; Gimondi won. Belgian catastrophe! It took thirty years for Merckx and Maertens to have a civil reconciliation.

While riding for the Flandria cycles team, Freddy found the factory bike frames to be too heavy and generally unworthy. He took a page out of Roger De Vlaeminck's book and had his frames built by Gios in Turin instead.[2] Maertens's *palmarès* is like Greg LeMond's in that they both won the World Championship title twice along with a multitude of Tour de France stages, yet neither

---

1 Alberic 'Briek' Schotte was another Flemish tough-guy racer. A man who trained so hard and so long in the worst weather he would forget what parish he had to ride home to. He knew everything about Belgian racing and was hard as nails. Who else would you want as your *directeur sportif*?

2 Roger De Vlaeminck, The Gypsy, Mr Paris–Roubaix, born in East Flanders, supremely talented, smooth-on-the-bike Hardman (see p. 107). He preceded Freddy on the Flandria team and was the first to have his bikes discreetly made by Gios. This business of stealth bike frames has been around for ages. Bicycle companies large enough to sponsor professional teams are often not adept at making the lightweight frames demanded by their very particular riders. Custom shops such as Jaegher in Flanders, Cyfac in France and Ben Serotta in the USA have produced many bikes for top professionals that were used under commercial camouflage.

Hey, Freddy. What say we start pushing on the pedals?

won a Monument. And though Maertens's Grand Tour record only extends to one title, to Greg's three, it was achieved in some style. In 1977 he won the Vuelta a España's opening prologue and pulled on the leader's jersey. He won half the following stages and never relinquished the jersey. Even Greg LeMond never ran the table like that.

If Freddy Maertens had had the single-minded drive of Eddy Merckx, he would have been Belgium's next king, but life's distractions proved too much for him. When he was good, he was brilliant; when he was bad, he couldn't finish a race. Alcoholism and financial troubles took a terrible toll and doubtless shortened his career. But still, with 373 professional wins that was quite a career.[3]

Freddy Maertens earned his Hardman status with his

---

3 The Belgians apparently like their career wins to be palindromes. Eddy finished with 525.

Hardman training, just like Sean Kelly, who followed him. It was their incredibly hard training that built the foundations for their racing successes. If Freddy's objective was a 270 km race, his training rides would be 300 km. If you have been training 30 extra kilometres every time you go out, you don't fear going hard to the finish of any race. That final hill, that last headwind flat. To be strong there, you need to have gone out training and barely made it home, again and again and again. We may lack the natural speed of Freddy Maertens, but if we train up properly, we can at least make sure we are there at the end.

Nowadays Freddy Maertens holds the post of curator of the Centrum Ronde van Vlaanderen in Oudenaarde, Belgium. It's good to know that Flanders looks after its own.

DJAMOLIDINE ABDOUJAPAROV

The Champ on the Champs

Well, this is awkward.

To the average Cyclist, professional sprinters are insane. The speeds they go and the risks they take are so terrifying they can only possibly be justified (and still only if you are indeed insane) by the number of victories possible; no one has a fatter *palmarès* than a champion sprinter.

Djamolidine Abdoujaparov, like Andrei Tchmil (see p. 133), was a Soviet youth selected for sports school at an early age.

The combination of an abundance of fast twitch muscles and an absolute lack of fear made him either the perfect potential sprinter or bare-handed Siberian bear killer. He went with the scarier career. He had a very good turn of speed. He did not mind contact at 60 kph. He was not 'into' holding his line.[1] Reckless and ruthless, his rivals quickly learned to give the Tashkent Terror some space.

It is impossible to describe accurately the speed and chaos of a Pro bunch sprint. And you can double that when you're talking about the Tour's final stage in Paris, on the Champs-Élysées. The single biggest sprint in the world. Every rider with some speed left in their legs wants this win more than life itself. In the 1991 Tour, Abdou was there in the sacred sprinter's green jersey. To win on the Champs-Élysées in the green jersey, yes, surely that is worth taking some risks for. As the sprinters fanned across the Champs, going top speed, there was Abdou, owning the right edge of the grand avenue, head down, giving it his all. Unfortunately his all included getting his wheels tangled up with the feet of the steel barriers and the giant Coca-Cola cans lining them. He crashed so hard we had to invent new expletives to express our shock.

Jonathan Vaughters, ex-Pro and team manager, tries to explain what a crash is like for a professional Cyclist by asking the non-cyclist to imagine opening their car door and jumping

---

1 Holding your line is in the top three things to *always* do as a Cyclist. It means maintaining a relatively consistent course, especially when others may be overtaking you. If you waver, you'll cause a crash, involving you, those overtaking Cyclists and even motorcycles, cars and spectators in a maelstrom of death, destruction and lost sunglasses. Hold your line! The other two things to always do: avoid touching your brakes when riding in a paceline with others close behind you. To ride 10 cm from another's rear wheel requires trust: trust the forward rider won't grab a handful of brakes and drop you to the pavement. And the other one? We forgot what it is, but it's really important.

out at 50 kph just sporting their budgie smugglers (our term, not his). Well, for an Abdou Champs crash, get your car up to 65 kph, and make sure you jump out into some road furniture.[2] Tumble a hundred feet while fellow Cyclists plough into you, with all their momentum concentrated into the width of their front wheel, and then lie there possibly dead for a while, for effect. If, when the paramedics come, you manage to deliver a cheeky Stephen Roche-style shagging joke, well, then you win the World. Which Abdou didn't. It took him twenty minutes to stagger across the finish line and into an ambulance, with the help of teammates. He had cracked ribs, a broken clavicle, internal injuries and a rumoured ruptured testicle. He was hurt – we can be sure that's not a rumour. He is the only jersey winner not to stand on the podium in Paris. All in a day's work for the Tashkent Terror.

Do you want to be that guy? We don't either. But then, you've got to Unleash Hell sometimes, right? We strongly recommend, however, that when Unleashing some Hell, you hold your line, occasionally watch where you're going and avoid all road furniture while you let your inner Abdou out.

---

2 Sounds comfy, doesn't it? But we're not talking upholstery here. We're talking traffic islands, bollards, all types of road architecture that is installed to keep traffic moving safely in opposite directions, and which becomes deadly hazardous when 120 Cyclists are hauling ass on *both* sides of it. The French motorcycle gendarmes are very good at alerting Cyclists about furniture. They stand, Moses-like, in front of it, parting the Red Sea of lycra and carbon fibre, by waving a little yellow flag. There is nothing between the gendarme and this sea of onrushing matter bar their moto leathers and a scant pair of French underwear. Respect.

SEAN KELLY, PART II

More Than Just a Pair of Legs

It is customary to talk about Kelly as a quintessentially Irish rider … For my part, though, I think it helps place Kelly better as a cyclist to see him as the last of the Flemish riders. This is a title usually associated with the post-war rider, Briek Schotte, who has become appropriately enough the man in the day-to-day charge of the de Gribaldy teams. As exemplified by Schotte it stood for a certain type of mentality: poor, willingness to suffer, narrowly focused and hard, hard, hard.

Robin Magowan, *Kings of the Road*

Sean Kelly was born into an Irish farming family. Forty-eight acres of crops, chickens, livestock and milk cows in Curragh-duff, County Waterford. What was on the dinner table depended on everyone's hard work out on the farm. Sean understood what working life was all about from an early age.

The moment he turned Pro was quintessentially Kelly; Flandria's team manager, Jean de Gribaldy, had flown up from France in his small plane to sign this little-known Irishman and literally had to stop a tractor on the road and ask, 'Are you Sean Kelly?' (It was.) At that moment Cycling became a way for Sean to earn a better living, if not an easier one. But it still took a few seasons of racing to convince Sean he could actually make it work. These were still the days of riders driving themselves to one-day races, bike on the roof or in the boot, like Merckx (bigger car). There were no team buses, no high-altitude training camps, no sports psychologists. You showed up at each start with your bike and kit and raced. Even after Kelly won his first Paris–Roubaix, his mud-caked bike sat in his garage until he was ready to clean it; he washed his own bike and oiled his own chain.

After the Tour de France there were marathon driving sessions around Europe to attend all the small-town post-Tour races. Meals were found at highway cafés, and journeys often went on until three in the morning. There were no beers, no cream with coffee. This was their trade, and this was how it was done. Big-name riders rode for the entry fee, and the winner was mostly decided beforehand. Kelly never missed an opportunity to earn some money doing this, even though he was the one doing both the racing *and* the driving. Much has been made of Sean's old-school, frugal ways. But he was there to win and to earn. He was not about pissing away money on sports cars or fancy houses. The professional Cyclist's career is, at best, fifteen years long, after all. He went to the Continent to earn a living: a decent bike, a good functional car, in bed by 9 p.m., training, always training. Sex before racing? No, never.

> My policy is to abstain for a week before a one-day classic and about six weeks before a major Tour.
>
> David Walsh, *A Biography of Sean Kelly*

When the young Greg LeMond arrived from the United States, Kelly was already a well-established continental star. While both were interlopers of sorts, Greg was all 'modern' Cycling while Sean was still doing his Cycling the traditional 'Euro' way. To the American, fresh on the European scene, all this old-school doctrine made little sense and was not to be believed or followed. Also, there were no burritos. *Don't these Euros realise how awesome burritos are?*[1]

Greg was by far the more naturally gifted rider. Kelly had a sprint, but it was sheer hard work and an iron will that accounted for his success. Which included more than a few of the greatest one-day races: nine Monuments to Greg's nil. It's a rare rider who can, as Kelly did, win Paris–Roubaix and Liège–Bastogne–Liège in the same month. If Sean hadn't gone to bed earlier than Greg, shagged less than Greg, eaten less than Greg and not trained with such single-minded hardness, he might not have had such a stellar career. It is this Hardman attitude, which he inherited as a farmer's son, that made his career what it was.

> When you train better, you become a better rider. You have to push yourself to the limit – that's what makes the top riders. Some people can't do it, but that's what makes the good ones and the great ones.
>
> Sean Kelly

Kelly's first Classic win was the 1983 Giro di Lombardy, now Il Lombardia, the last big race of the season, hence dubbed the Race of the Falling Leaves. He had won the amateur version but six years into his professional career had not managed a single big one-day title, let alone one of the Monuments of Cycling (see Glossary). Even his *directeur sportif*, Jean de Gribaldy, said Sean couldn't handle the pressure to win a *real* race. (Thanks, de Grib.) Sean was beset by self-doubt these six years, but at Lombardy his teammates and a fellow Irishman from another team were ready to back him.

The Tour of Lombardy is a rambling, hilly race. It's hard from

---

1 Greg LeMond was known for his love of American ways and Mexican food. It has been alleged that one night on the Tour de France, he, his wife Kathy and fellow American Andy Hampsten hijacked their hotel kitchen to make themselves a load of burritos. Burritos rule!

the start and relentless to the finish, as it circumnavigates the picturesque Lake Como. Coming so late in the season, it attracts a mix of riders, some hoping for redemption and others burned out, just looking to end their racing obligations for the year. Many a rider is looking for a seat in the team car at the first feed zone. With thirty-six miles to the finish, three-quarters of the field was off the back. But the lead group was still too big for comfort, so Kelly's Swiss teammate Jean-Marie Grezet went to the front. Grezet methodically burned through all his matches to keep the pace high. Twenty-eight miles later his last match went out, and the attacks began. With no teammates left, Kelly could not contain them. He did, though, have fellow Irishman Stephen Roche with him in the break. Roche was certainly not Kelly's teammate and was there to ride for his team captain, the Australian Phil Anderson.

> I rode hard at the front to keep it together. Kelly hadn't asked me to help, he just glanced over in my direction and it was up to me. I wanted to do it for him because we were good friends and I knew he needed to win a classic ... After the race my Peugeot manager Roland Berland was angry because I had ridden for Kelly. Berland just didn't understand. OK I helped Kelly to win but I wasn't going well enough to win myself. There would be other days when the roles would be reversed. Sean has always been an honest and straight rider, he would repay the debt.
>
> Stephen Roche

Their last climb done with, the remaining group of eighteen was led into Como by Roche. This was going to be a sprint, and Italy's best hope now rested with Francesco Moser: big, powerful but not a true sprinter. Stephen Roche still led under the *flamme rouge* – the 1-Kilometre-To-Go banner – and he used every ounce of his remaining power to give Sean the best lead-out he had:

*Adri van der Poel, Kelly, LeMond and Hennie Kuiper. Moser
is behind Kelly and Stephen Roche back there, somewhere.*

I had worked very hard. It was all for Sean. [Hennie] Kuiper went past
me and I expected Sean to follow soon. I mean we were entering the
finishing straight. But all these other fellows came by before Kelly. I
wondered what he was playing at. Wondered had I been working for
nothing? I counted them as they passed, about eight or nine before
Kelly went by.

Stephen Roche

Kelly went by with Greg LeMond glued to his wheel. As they
approached the finish line, Greg started to pass, and bikes were
thrown.[2] Four finishers spread across the road, with Kelly the
first over the line.

The 1983 Tour of Lombardy win was Kelly's first huge win.
He went back home to Ireland knowing he really could beat the

———————————————

2 An effort to put your front tyre across the line first by thrusting your
bars forwards with your arms. Timing the throw perfectly can win you a
close sprint.

best. Winter training in Ireland was wet and cold and windy, but that had never bothered Sean. And now he knew it was worth it. What can we do to be more like King Kelly? Get some kilometres in while others are peering out the window. Embrace Rule #9, train in shiet weather and channel your inner badass.[3]

---

3 Rule #9, *If you are out riding in bad weather, it means you are a badass. Period.* Riding in cold rain empowers you. As the rain drips off your casquette brim, you are almost Eddy Merckx. And you get to add to your bad-weather Cycling wardrobe: win-win.

ROBBIE McEWEN

July 2007

Professional sprinters are a rare breed. Typically confident, usually fiery, sometimes cocky, necessarily fearless. Bumping elbows at 60 kph is not for most professionals, whose livelihood is generally reliant on staying in one piece. When punches are thrown and heads butted at that speed, well, that's just the sprinters sorting things out among themselves. When the crashes, the road rash, the fractures and ambulance rides get too much, it's time for a sprinter to re-jig their career. Laurent Jalabert, Kelly, Museeuw, Boonen: all started out as specialist sprinters, then, as they got older, wiser and a bit slower, branched out to find other ways to win. Others just kept sprinting, like Robbie McEwen.

Robbie made the voyage from his native Australia to race in Europe and settled in the Flemish Ardennes. He was too small to bump shoulders with the big heavyweights, but he had an abundance of speed and fearlessness and an uncanny ability to be in just the right place at the right time to win, a lot. He usually counted on a single teammate to get him close to the front, and then he did the rest. No sprint trains for Robbie.

The 1997 Tour de France's first stage, in the UK, was a sprinter's stage, no question. It was flat, with a fast run-in to the finish in Canterbury. The old guard was represented by Eric Zabel, the new by neo-Pro Mark Cavendish (who would go on to finish ten Grand Tours and counting, amassing forty-eight stage wins). Between them, McEwen was at the height of his powers. He had won eleven Tour de France stages, and he wanted to make this his twelfth. Sprint stages in the Grand Tours can be seen as formulaic: a non-threatening break is allowed to escape, then is eventually reeled back in with enough time for a giant, high-speed fireworks display of a sprint to be lit, ending in a pyrotechnic display of lead-out trains, crashes, frustrated handlebar hammering and various tasteless victory salutes. The speed the pack goes in the last half-hour of a sprinting stage starts insane and just keeps getting insaner. Poor young Cavendish never even got there; he tangled with a spectator just as the pace started to get high, and hit the deck. By the time he had changed wheels and bikes, he was riding in by himself for 186th place. Not exactly how he had imagined his first Tour de France stage finish.

In a separate accident Robbie hit the deck too. Unlike Cav, McEwen kept his cool. Four teammates dropped back and started to drag him back to the peloton. While McEwen's team were alerted to get to the back, every other sprinter's team got to the front. The best way to ensure Robbie didn't beat you in the sprint was to make sure he didn't even make it to the sprint. Tom Boonen's Quick Step team massed on the front and accelerated the previously insane pace to hyper-insane. With 5 km to go, Robbie's teammates had buried themselves to get their captain on to the back of the now single-file field. But this close to the finish, the back of the field was a long way from the front of the field, and the speed was just too high for anyone to move up.

The final field sprint was a blur of blue jerseys as Zabel and Boonen's trains burned through their fast men. South Africa's Robbie Hunter jumped early, then died early. At the last second Robbie McEwen bumped shoulders with a Soudal rider and then simply launched off the front, all the way to the line. He had no lead-out train or even a single teammate; he had stormed up

All in a day's work, at 70 kmph.

through the field with just enough strength to burst out from the front with 50 metres left.

This was a singular feat, this win number twelve, and one would imagine it was Robbie's sweetest Tour de France win. Never saying, 'I'm done for today', but instead saying, 'I'm still in this!' This is the embodiment of a Hardman. Actual Belgians like Boonen must have wondered, 'What else do we have to do to beat that wily Aussie?' Hardmen all possess this unwillingness to quit, ever. From Beryl Burton to Robbie McEwen, quitting was not in their souls, so try to keep it out of yours; the measure of a Cyclist is taken at the finish line, so make sure you cross it. Unfortunately for us, we can't sprint like Cav or McEwen, They picked their fast-twitching parents wisely. But lucky for us too, we don't have to contest every town line sprint by head-butting, elbowing and inevitably crashing with our friends at too many kilometres per hour. Another lesson for us civilians is: don't prejudge the little guy who looks fourteen (Robbie) or the old bastard whose knees stick out, or even the fat bastard with hairy legs. They might just be faster than you. Judge them first by how they ride their bike, then how they look on their bike. If they do both really well then that, we suppose, is something.

FINALE

You have three questions going through your mind:
How far to go?
How hard am I trying?
Is the pace sustainable for that distance?
If the answer is 'yes', that means you're not trying hard enough. If it's no, it's too late to do anything about it. You're looking for the answer 'maybe'.

Chris Boardman on the Hour Record, *Rouleur*

The question we must all ask ourselves whenever that little voice starts going on about how hard it is, or how much it hurts or how easy it would be to stop the suffering just by easing off the gas a touch (which is 'little voice' code for 'a lot') is how much the knowledge that we quit will bother us when the 2 a.m. Ghost of Lost Opportunities comes knocking. We've already discussed the main problem with quitting: it keeps getting easier to do; the more we do it, the more we adjust to the feeling and the more accustomed we become to the idea of quitting. The baby freshly liberated from its mother's womb knows nothing of quitting; it knows only to cry in order to evacuate its lungs of all that spooge it's been breathing in during its gestation. There is no choice: only the fight for survival.

Quitting is learned. It is a luxury born of our status at the top of the food chain. Every other living thing on the planet is engaged in a life-or-death fight for its individual rung on the ladder of evolution except for us humans. We finished fighting that fight ages ago, thanks to the tools and weapons we could conjure up with our giant brains. Ever since, our species has been lounging in a virtual poolside deckchair, sipping a drink with an umbrella in it. Lots of people still suffer in this world; survival is no joke. But most of us have it pretty easy – at least, most of us who are reading this book. (And those of you who read every word, you suffered a little more than the rest.) For us, Cycling means choosing to be tough, taking the harder path, fighting for something that matters to us. And it makes us fit and healthy, which is the greatest side-effect possible. Most things that are fun make you fat or give you diseases. Not Cycling. And: beer is officially a 'recovery beverage'! Best. Sport. In. The. World.

Having finished this book (if you have), you may be asking yourself how is it possible we left out some of the most hardened, tough riders in the world? There are a variety of explanations, some of which include things like 'would have required research' or 'forgot about them until after we finished'. Both of which are completely legitimate reasons. But we will take a moment to point out a few omissions and give our justifications, just to humour you (because, in truth, we don't care, and if you want an argument, you know where we are – join the queue).

Tom Boonen. Total stud, Hardman, probably the finest *klassieker* the sport will ever know. He won a record-tying four Paris–Roubaix, and came unbearably close to winning his fifth in 2016. By the time you read this, we'll know if he won his fifth in 2017. The problem with Tommeke is that there is so much to love about him that we couldn't settle on what to cover, and it would take up an entire book to discuss him properly. What a stud.

Hennie Kuiper. Dutchman. That's almost enough on its own. Being the only rider we can think of (besides Fausto Coppi) without trying very hard ('research', remember?) who has won both Paris–Roubaix and L'Alpe d'Huez is a singularly incredible feat, one that will not be repeated in our current generation of specialisation. But again, the drunken arguments betwixt Keepers regarding which chapter he should be included in – *rouleurs, grimpeurs* or *klassiekers* – yielded a stalemate, and by the time we sobered up we forgot about it and wrote about someone else instead.

Greg LeMond. How can we leave him out? Three Tours de France, two World Championships, total stud. He was also uniquely open to the press regarding his various grievances, which made him both endearing and annoying. If only he were French, then we wouldn't even have noticed.

Fabian Cancellara. Two words: his complaint about including cobbles in the Tour de France. As an undeniable master of the cobbles, he was enthusiastic about their inclusion prior to the start of the stage. Afterwards, however, when his team leader lost a heap of time over the stones, he complained that they shouldn't be in a Grand Tour. Apparently the Tour should only include climbs.

Alberto Contador. In his later years he has developed into a much more charismatic and enigmatic racer, but his early years were full of arrogance and his Grand Tour wins were largely uninteresting, following the formulas made popular by Lance Pharmstrong.

Chris Froome. Boring, and Team Sky has adopted the same excitement-smothering tactics made popular by Lance Armstrong's US Postal and Discovery teams, 2016 aside. Looks like a spider humping a light bulb on a bike. Very unfortunate.

Chris Boardman. Time trial stud. Hour Record hero. His account in *Rouleur* of what his 'Merckx-style' Hour ride was like is worthy of being set in bronze and mounted high atop Mount Velomis. We aren't opposed to plagiarising, but only when our plagiarisms are better than what we're copying from. And that bit is a masterpiece, so we refer you there instead.

Graeme Obree. Possibly the hardest, certainly the most innovative, Cyclist ever. His efforts at the Hour and his rivalry with Boardman made for one of the most exciting and interesting periods of modern Cycling. His story is too complicated to tell in this context, and we refer you again to his own autobiography.

The list goes on: there are too many to document. If you

disagree with our selections, we invite/dare you to join the 'con-versation' at Velominati.com and make your case.

We hope you enjoyed the book. Now put it away and go ride your bike. We are Cyclists. The rest of the world merely rides a bike. Vive la Vie Velominatus.

GLOSSARY

See also 'The Lexicon' on the Veominati, which is based similarly on our fancy and is therefore equally incomplete and contradictory.

Belleville effect // *The Triplets of Belleville*, a French film actually called *Belleville Rendez-vous* (which doesn't mean 'The Triplets of Belleville' at all), is a must-see animated Cycling film where the riders have disproportionately large guns but spindly upper bodies. In other words, they look exactly how each of us Cyclists see ourselves.

Bergs **(or** *hellingen***) //** An irregular and Englishified pluralisation of the Dutch (Flemish) word *berg*, which means 'mountain'. *Hellingen* means 'hills'. When you're hypoxic, hills often start to feel like mountains, so that's probably where the confusion came from. In any case, these brutes are abrupt, steep, often cobbled hills found in the Flemish Ardennes in Belgium. These usually lie in wait just after a quick right or left off a main road, surprising the unsuspecting rider with their brutishness.

Big Ring, The // aka *la plaque*, the big dog or, if you are an old-school Flandrian, your only chainring. In Flanders, they come in 55-, 54- and 53-tooth configurations. The only reason a Belgian even has an inner chainring is as their contingency plan for if they break the outer one on some dirty cobble. Pro tip: riding in the small chainring makes you go slower.

Braze // Artisanal steel bike-frame-building technique. No one in the factory who built your top-shelf carbon frame will have a clue what to do with one of these, but if you break your steel frame in a deserted town, even the local plumber should be able to help you with an emergency repair.

Broom wagon // The bus that follows the race at the minimum allowed speed, scooping up broken riders and ferrying them to the finish. It lurks at the back of the race, reminding everyone that, if it passes them, they are then either going to be riding on alone, for pride, or climbing into the bus for the journey to the finish, reflecting on how soft they are. Imagine the torture for the broken rider who hears the pitter-patter of the broom wagon's motor coming ever closer. Agony.

Burning matches // At the beginning of each race you start with a full box of matches. Every effort you make is referred to as burning a match, so every time you chase someone down, or chase back from a puncture, or put your face into the wind, you burn a match and once you've used them all up, you're finished. The only place you can get more matches from is at the bottom of a bowl of pasta or buried somewhere in your mattress, appearing only after a sound sleep. How well you save and use your matches determines your result. Use them too quickly and you're fucked. Don't use them quickly enough and the race has already disappeared up the road. The split-second decision to burn your last match is what often decides the race. Cycling analogies for fatigue are endless: running on fumes, smoking like a hippie's motorbike, cracked, *un jour sans*, and the much-used Liggettism, being in a spot of bother.

Cannibal // Eddy Merckx's nickname, which he himself apparently dislikes. The people eater, the man who eats his competition alive. Maybe he just doesn't like the colour purple?

Chapeau // French for 'I doff my hat to you, good sir.' Sounds infinitely more sophisticated than simply saying 'hat'.

Cobble trophy // The winner of Paris–Roubaix gets a granite cobblestone on a plinth. Lifting it is quite a workout for a Cyclist's traditionally feeble, Mr Burns-like arms, which have additionally just been shaken halfway to destruction on just such cobbles.

Convertible casquette // A cap for hot days when some shade for the face would be nice. It involves cutting the dome off a cotton cap, leaving the wee bill for shade but an open top for heat loss and for flowing locks of hair, should the rider be fortunate enough not to be bald.

COTHO // Oft-quoted acronym, which doesn't *quite* stand for Chap Of The Highest Order, but we'll look forward to seeing you next Tuesday. Originally applied to a certain Texan, it spread throughout the annals of the Velominati and has been applied to many other pedigreed dopers who display a certain *chappiness*. Doping alone is not a sufficient qualification for COTHO status: a true COTHO will display other classic traits such as being Texan, riding a Trek, possessing beady blue eyes that are way too close together and being named Lance. Being a chronic Rule 43-breaker is usually also sufficient cause for COTHO status.

Criterium // Fast and furious circuit race, characteristic of North American bike-racing. The races are measured in a combination of time and laps (i.e. forty-five minutes to the bell, then three more laps) and are generally designed to appeal to crowds more than the classical road race. Similar but not related to the Flemish and Dutch *kermis*, which is a circuit race held, originally, around the perimeter of a carnival (*kermis*) ground.

Crown // The pronounced hump down the centre of a French cobbled road. Centuries of ox carts and farm machinery have formed it, pushing the stones and earth under the wheels of the cart down into the gutter. It is not typically smoother, but it is safer: drier, with no puddles and fewer surprises. The strong riders tend to ride the crown, for this reason, while the weaker ones will dive down into the gutter in search of smoother, faster passage. The risk there being that of punctures, as all the debris from the crown has been washed down into the gutter by the rains that fall endlessly in this part of Europe.

Directeur sportif // A French term for the guy who sits in the team car and tells his riders what to do. Unless that rider was Eddy Merckx, in which case he was the guy who sat in the team car getting yelled at by Eddy Merckx. No one told Eddy what to do.

Domestiques // Teammates who ride in service of their leader and thus rarely win races themselves. They spend hours on the front of the bunch, laying down The V, in order to reel in a breakaway or to crush the will of rival teams by keeping the pace unrelentingly high on the run-in to the finale or the base of the final climb.

Drilling it // Riding at or near your anaerobic threshold, as hard as you can. Similar: pushing hard on the pedals, crushing it, giving it the berries, ripping the legs off, nailing it, on the rivet, *à bloc*, full gas, in the red, beasting it (UK only), majorly suffering (Sean Kelly only).

Drop // The vertical distance between saddle and handlebars. As David Millar said, 'A bike's got to look good just sitting there, doesn't it?' Drop is what makes a bike look good, kids. Like 'showing post', this is something the civilian maximises in order to look more Pro. As with the showing of post, it has resulted in a lot of people with handlebars so low they never ride in the drops. Which is known as a Sub Optimal Outcome.

Five and Nine // Shorthand for Rule #5 (Harden the Fuck Up) and Rule #9 (If you are out riding in bad weather, it means you're a badass. Period).

Flahute // A *flahute* is the word the Flemish use to describe the *really* tough riders. Someone once told us that Tom Boonen trains on the Koppenberg by riding it in the 53. Tom Boonen is a *flahute*.

Flamme rouge // Banner or arch over the road with a red flag marking 1 kilometre to the finish; the Red Kite, if you insist on referring to things by their English name. Many a last-ditch effort to win the race has been launched from this point and just as many dreams have been crushed where the day-long breakaway is reeled in just as the bunch rides under the banner.

Flandrian // A native of Flanders, Belgium, where even small children ride in the big ring and bike races aren't called bike races unless half the starters don't make it to the finish line.

Grand Tour // Three-week stage races, of which there are only three – one each for France (the Tour de France), Italy (il Giro d'Italia), and Spain (La Vuelta a España). *Flahutes* refer to them as three weeks of training rides.

Grande Boucle Féminine Internationale // The women's Tour de France – or one version of it, at any rate – held from 1984 until 2009. In its heyday it shared the final podium presentation with the men on the Champs-Élysées, but then suffered organisational and funding challenges that led to its demise.

Gregario // Italian for Cycling *domestique*, but, as the word implies, a *gregario* is a compatriot, a friend in the trenches, not just a worker.

Guns // The legs of the Cyclist, their primary (and only) weapon. Also cannons, howitzers, The Last Argument of Kings according to Louis XIV, who had it engraved in Latin (*Ultima ratio regum*) on his artillery pieces – a practice that the celebrated author Chris Cleave has suggested the committed Cyclist might adopt with his or her **Big Ring**. It is obligatory to compare one's quadriceps (not biceps; we are Cyclists not, as we may have mentioned already, savages who go about punching each other or lifting weighty objects) to military tools of death and destruction. For example: 'Did you hear the guns of Navarone echoing across the valley yesterday afternoon? That was me on the golf course hill.'

Hairnet // The protective headwear of the '70s, compulsory in Belgium until the hardshell helmet was stylish enough to be accepted into the peloton. Not quite a helmet, it offered a *bit* more protection than a cotton cap. The hairnet was made of leather and stuffed with ... something, possibly horsehair. It looked badass, full stop. When worn over a cotton Cycling cap, it looked even badasser. Did it protect skulls? Let's just agree it looked badass.

Hell of the North // The semi-official nickname of **Paris–Roubaix**, originally because of its route through war-ruined landscape left over by the Maginot Line. More recently, more because of the Been-to-Hell-and-Back expressions on the faces of the finishers.

Holding your line // Referring specifically to the practice of riding in a straight line, but more generally to the art of riding predictably and consistently in the group. People who walk in crowds while texting generally demonstrate through antithesis the value of holding your line.

Keepers (of the Cog) // The five principal authors of the Velominati: Frank Strack, Gianni Andrews, Brett Kennedy, Marko Carlson and Jim Thomson.

Kermesse // Dutch and Flemish circuit races originally held around the property of the local carnival, a *kermis*. See **Criterium**.

Laughing group // The *gruppetto*; a group of riders joined together in bleak solidarity at the back of the race, attempting to finish before the time limit, typically calculated as a certain percentage over the stage winner's time. The broom wagon rides at this speed; if a rider misses the time limit, they are eliminated from the race altogether. This concept generally only applies to stage races where the riders care about starting again the next day. The laughing group usually contains a few riders who are masters of calculating exactly how fast they need to ride in order to make the time limit. Erik Zabel was one of these riders, to whom the non-mathematically inclined riders (most of them) would look for leadership in setting the tempo.

Maglia rosa // The leader's jersey for the Giro d'Italia. The Tours of Italy and France were both started by newspapers, and in both cases they chose the colour for the leader's jersey from the colour of the newsprint they used; where *L'Auto* used yellow paper, *La Gazetta dello Sport* used pink.

Magnificent stroke // A rider's smooth, powerful stroke. *Pedal stroke*.

Maillot jaune // Yellow jersey, worn by the race leader in the Tour de France. Wearing this for one day bestows a certain amount of honour for the rest of one's life.

Man with the Hammer, The // He stalks all Cyclists. He cannot be outridden or avoided. Everyone meets him eventually, and everyone remembers him. Ride long enough and hard enough and there he will be, hammer cocked, boom, out go the lights. You are now riding in slow motion, children are running easily alongside, laughing and mocking. Congratulations, you have just met The Man with the Hammer.

Marginal gains // The concept of many very small improvements combined over time to bring success. Brought into popularity by Team Sky and now brought into question due to concerns over their use of Therapeutic Use Exemptions.

Monument // Like a golf Major (what is golf?) or a Grand Slam tournament in tennis (but way harder, and with less grunting), one of the big five Classic races: Milano–Sanremo, Ronde van Vlaanderen, Paris–Roubaix, Liège–Bastogne–Liège and Giro di Lombardia. Winning one ensures Legend status for the rider, even if that's all they ever win.

Moto // A motorcycle carrying a gendarme, photographer, TV cameraperson or French ex-Pro *avec* microphone doing live commentary during a bike race. The race is surrounded by a swarm of motorcycles buzzing in all directions, and the motorcycle pilots (drivers) are very good. It is stressful and dangerous work, but they do wear leather from head to toe instead of Lycra, and they have a throttle. They also tend to get in the way of the race and cause crashes and much cursing in foreign languages.

Mountain goat // A term used to describe that annoying breed of Cyclist who insists on going uphill much too quickly for everyone else. These are some of the most graceful riders when the road points uphill, a skill apparently not always communicative with going downhill.

Musette // The cotton throwaway lunch bag handed off to riders part-way through a race so they can eat on the bike. They are snatched at speed and looped over the head; contents are inspected for insertion into jersey pocket, immediate inhalation or immediate ejection. Many a rider has come to grief at the 'feed zone', where bidons fire sideways from the peloton like decoy flares from a military transport in a war zone.

Neo-Pro // A first-year professional, the one who is now experiencing the abrupt transition to higher speeds and longer distances. And going from winning all the under-23 amateur races to finishing last, if at all.

Neutralised // The first few kilometres of a race is normally 'neutralised' as it leaves a busy town centre. The peloton rides patiently behind the race commissar's car until the signal is given that the real race has begun. Normally followed by a Frenchman attacking immediately.

Omertà // The code of silence, of non-cooperation with authorities and interference in the actions of those who attempt to expose illegal activities. As it was with the Cosa Nostra, it has become the peloton's version of *see no evil, hear no evil, speak no evil.*

On the rivet // Old Brooks leather saddles were riveted together with one rivet on the nose and several across the back. When a rider is going full gas, they inexplicably and inexorably slide towards the nose of the saddle; in those days, to be 'on the rivet' was to be perched on the front of your saddle, sitting on the top of the little brass rivet, and today we still use the expression because it sounds sexier than 'on the leather nose of the saddle'.

Packing // Yorkshire for abandoning a race.

Palmarès // French for a rider's list of wins and placings. Sounds cooler than 'CV'.

Paniagua // *Faux*-Spanish term for 'bread and water', used to mean riding without medical enhancement.

Panzerwagen // German for armoured car and every language for Tony Martin. See p. 146.

Parcours // The classic Cycling term referring to the profile of a race route. Why don't we just say 'profile'? Because *'parcours'* is French and it is customary to adopt the old European terms for such things whenever possible in order to mystify our sport further to those not familiar with it. Compare use of *'terroir'* in wine. Also not to be confused with the relatively new sport wherein people jump around an urban landscape like uncaged monkeys.

Paris–Roubaix // Possibly the hardest single-day race of the year. One of the five Monuments of racing. It takes place in northern France on the second Sunday in April, and winning it requires equal amounts of strength and bike handling. Whole books have been written on just this race. It is a race for Hardmen.

Paris–Tours // A semi-Classic race run every autumn. It does not start in Paris, but it does end in Tours, often in a big sprint. No books have been written on just this race and it is not only for Hardmen, although they do often participate and sometimes even win it.

Passista // Italian for *rouleur*. See p. 51.

Pavé // French for cobblestones. These are not the cobblestones you have in your town plaza. These are brutish beasts that make up the secteurs of Paris–Roubaix, many of them laid by Napoleon or even the Romans. There is a group in France called Les Amis de Paris–Roubaix, whose function is to maintain, preserve and restore these ancient roads, so that they stay just the right side of completely un-fucking-rideable.

Polka dot jersey // AKA *le maillot à pois rouges*, the dotty jumper. It is the jersey worn by the leader in the King of the Mountains (KOM) contest in the Tour de France where riders accumulate points by crossing designated high points on a day's course in first, second, third and so on. It is also the cause of many riders with poor taste in aesthetics wearing dotted bib shorts and riding dotted bikes. Please stop this trend immediately.

Post-Tour criterium // Exhibition-style races held in provincial towns around Europe after the Tour. Traditionally, more emphasis is put on the big stars being visible and the local hero somehow winning than on strict sporting ethics. In other words, they are rigged: deals are done, alliances are made and results contrived. Adorable in their own way.

Prophet, The // Eddy Merckx, *bien sûr*.

Red egg // A little red candy-like pill which is actually testosterone. Sounds delicious.

Road furniture // A comfortable-sounding description for something that can cause major bodily harm to Cyclist and spectator alike. Very popular in northern Europe. Traffic islands, bollards, all the road architecture installed to keep traffic moving safely in opposite directions which becomes deathly hazardous when 120 Cyclists are hauling ass on *both* sides of it.

Ronde van Vlaanderen // The Ronde, The Tour of Flanders, Belgium's Big Day. Bigger than Christmas, it is, along with Paris–Roubaix, arguably the hardest one-day race of the year. It is long, and almost every climb is a cobbled, steep bottleneck. The positioning race to get to the foot of each *berg* is hellish, like a bunch sprint. If you arrive at a crucial climb halfway back in the peloton, your race is over.

Rooster tail // The watery spray from the rear wheel of a bicycle in the rain. Far from being a refreshing spritz of rainwater, it is a gritty mess filled with whatever lies on the road: sand, manure and all manner of things best left to the imagination.

Royce // English manufacturer specialising in forging hubs and bottom brackets. Royce has a terribly small following, given the quality of its work, but those who use its parts are loyal beyond explanation.

Rouleur // French for *Passista*. See p. 51.

Secteur // French for 'sector', referring to cobbled sections, usually anywhere from 1 to 3 km, making up the decisive bits of Paris–Roubaix. It is customary for the amateur Cyclist to shout 'SECTEUR' at the top of their lungs upon entering a section of *pavé*. It is unclear what the professional Cyclist shouts.

Showing post // Exposing a long section of seat post above the seat tube, as in: 'that dude is showing some serious post.' Probably used as phallic compensation.

Souplesse // Smoothness, suppleness, specifically of pedalling.

Another example of the fantastic and translation-resistant French Cycling language. Like the Buddha said in reference to enlightenment, the development of *souplesse* may take thirty lifetimes or thirty years.

Sprint train // Pioneered, or at least brought close to perfection, by the Italian Stallion Mario Cipollini. This tactic involves putting a number of very strong, fast *domestiques* and *rouleurs* directly in front of the sprinter in the closing kilometres of a race, cranking the speed up so high that no one can attack off the front any more. Each *rider* pulls for a few hundred metres and then peels off and coasts into the finish line while the next rider in line takes over at the front. The final rider would be the true lead-out rider, going insanely fast to deliver the sprinter at just the right moment, with, say, a hundred metres to go. The speed is so high that no one can come past, and boom: check out that sweet victory salute!

Stelvio // Passo dello Stelvio, a fabled, looping ribbon of switchbacks up to a pass in the Dolomites.

Sur la plaque // French for 'Put that thing in the **Big Ring**, fucktard.' (*Plaque* meaning 'plate', get it?)

Throwing the bike // Pushing (throwing) your bike forward with your arms at the end of a sprint. The equivalent of a runner's plunge for the tape. You break the line with the front edge of your front tyre, so thrusting your bike forward at just the right moment can win you a sprint. Many a bike race has been won by a well-timed throw.

Time bonus // Time, in seconds, awarded for stage finish placing or mid-race sprints.

Time cut // One of stage racing's harshest rules is the time limit for finishing each day's route, even in time trials, calculated by a percentage of the winning rider's time. It varies slightly depending on the type and severity of the stage but tends to be 15 to 20 per cent more than the winner's time. Finishing outside this time results in a rider's disqualification, so when some freak of nature like Pantani goes ape-shiet uphill, everyone at the back of the race has to get very busy not being eliminated. Cycling is cruel. So much so, in fact, that sometimes the race jury has pity on the broken rider who missed the limit if they are sufficiently heroic in their efforts.

UCI // Union Cycliste Internationale, Cycling's governing body. Sometimes referred to as the Union Cycliste Irrationale; the sort of bureaucratic organisation that hinders more than it governs. It turned a blind eye to the rampant doping that took place in Cycling during the 1990s and 2000s but felt compelled to limit the innovation that was taking place in bicycle technology, a position it has somewhat reversed by allowing time trial bikes back into the Hour Record.

V, The // Shorthand for the Velominati's all-important Rule #5: 'Harden the Fuck Up' (see Rules, p. 207). The power of The V or The Five surrounds us, penetrates us and holds us together. Not unlike The Force, in fact, although it won't help you aim your photon torpedoes.

Witch with Green Teeth, The // The French equivalent of **The Man with the Hammer**. She lurks in the shadows and swoops in to cause a sudden and catastrophic failure in the engine room. Sounds scarier than The Man with the Hammer.

THE RULES

Rule #1 // Obey The Rules.

Rule #2 // Lead by example.
It is forbidden for someone familiar with The Rules knowingly to assist another person to breach them.

Rule #3 // Guide the uninitiated.
No matter how good you think your reason is to breach The Rules, it is never good enough.

Rule #4 // It's all about the bike.
It is, absolutely, without question, unequivocally, about the bike. Anyone who says otherwise is obviously a twatwaffle.

Rule #5 // Harden the Fuck Up.

Rule #6 // Free your mind and your legs will follow.
Your mind is your worst enemy. Do all your thinking before you start riding your bike. Once the pedals start to turn, wrap yourself in the sensations of the ride – the smell of the air, the sound of the tyres, the feeling of flight as the bicycle rolls over the road.

Rule #7 // Tan lines should be cultivated and kept razor-sharp.
Under no circumstances should one be rolling up one's sleeves or shorts in an effort somehow to diminish one's tan lines. Sleeveless jerseys are under no circumstances to be employed.

Rule #8 // Saddles, bars and tyres shall be carefully matched.
Valid options are:

- Match the saddle to the bars and the tyres to black; or
- Match the bars to the colour of the frame at the top of the head tube and the saddle to the colour of the frame at the top of the seat tube and the tyres to the colour where they come closest to the frame; or
- Match the saddle and the bars to the frame decals; or
- Black, black, black

Rule #9 // If you are out riding in bad weather, it means you are a badass. Period.
Fair-weather riding is a luxury reserved for Sunday afternoons and wide boulevards. Those who ride in foul weather – be it cold, wet or inordinately hot – are members of a special club of riders who, on the morning of a big ride, pull back the curtain to check the weather and, upon seeing rain falling from the skies, allow a wry smile to spread across their face. This is a rider who loves the work.

Rule #10 // It never gets easier, you just go faster.
As this famous quote by Greg LeMan tells us, training, climbing and racing are hard. They stay hard. To put it another way, per Greg Henderson: 'Training is like fighting with a gorilla. You don't stop when you're tired. You stop when the gorilla is tired.' *Sur la plaque*, fucktards.

Rule #11 // Family does not come first. The bike does.
Sean Kelly, being interviewed after the '84 Amstel Gold Race, spots his wife leaning against his Citroën AX. He interrupts the interview to tell her to get off the paintwork, to which she shrugs, 'In your life the car comes first, then the bike, then me.' Instinctively, he snaps back: 'You got the order wrong. The bike comes first.'

Rule #12 // The correct number of bikes to own is n+1.
While the minimum number of bikes one should own is three, the correct number is n+1, where n is the number of bikes currently owned. This equation may also be rewritten as s−1, where s is the number of bikes owned that would result in separation from your partner.

Rule #13 // If you draw race number 13, turn it upside down.
Paradoxically, the same mind that holds such control over the body is also woefully fragile and prone to superstitious thought. It fills easily with doubt and is distracted by ancillary details. This is why the tape must always be perfect, the machine silent, the kit spotless. And, if you draw the unlucky number 13, turn it upside down to counteract its negative energy.

Rule #14 // Shorts should be black.[1]
Team-issue shorts should be black, with the possible exception of side-panels, which may match the rest of the team kit.

Rule #15 // Black shorts should also be worn with leader's jerseys.
Black shorts, or at least standard team-kit shorts, must be worn with Championship jerseys and race leadership jerseys. Don't over-match your kit, or accept that you will look like a douche.

Rule #16 // Respect the jersey.
Championship and race leadership jerseys must only be worn if you've won the championship or led the race.

Rule #17 // Team kit is for members of the team.
Wearing Pro team kit is also questionable if you're not paid to

---

1 Rule #14 was intentionally broken for the cover of this book. Live with it.

wear it. If you must fly the colours of Pro teams, all garments should match perfectly: e.g. no Mapei jersey with Kelme shorts and Telekom socks.

Rule #18 // Know what to wear. Don't suffer kit confusion.
No baggy shorts and jerseys while riding the road bike. No Lycra when riding the mountain bike (unless racing XC). Skin suits only for cyclocross.

Rule #19 // Introduce yourself.
If you deem it appropriate to join a group of riders who are not part of an open group ride and who are not your mates, it is customary and courteous to announce your presence. Introduce yourself and ask if you may join the group. If you have been passed by a group, wait for an invitation, introduce yourself or let them go. The silent joiner is viewed as ill mannered and Anti-V. Conversely, the joiner who can't shut their cakehole is no better and should be dropped from the group at first opportunity.

Rule #20 // There are only three remedies for pain.
These are:

- If your quads start to burn, shift forward to use your hamstrings and calves; or
- If your calves or hamstrings start to burn, shift back to use your quads; or
- If you feel wimpy and weak, meditate on Rule #5 and train more!

Rule #21 // Cold weather gear is for cold weather.
Knickers, vests, arm warmers, shoe covers and caps beneath your helmet can all make you look like a Hardman, when the weather warrants their use. If it isn't wet or cold, save your Flandrian Best for Flemish weather.

Rule #22 // Cycling caps are for Cycling.
Cycling caps can be worn under helmets, but never when not riding, no matter how hip you think you look. This will render one a douche, and should result in public berating or beating. The only time it is acceptable to wear a Cycling cap is while directly engaged in Cycling activities and while clad in Cycling kit. This includes activities taking place prior to and immediately after the ride such as machine tuning and tyre pumping. Also included are café appearances for pre-ride *espressi* and post-ride pub appearances for body-refuelling ales (provided said pub has sunny, outdoor patio – do not stray inside a pub wearing kit or risk being ceremoniously beaten by leather-clad biker chicks). Under these conditions, having your cap skull-side tipped jauntily at a rakish angle is, one might say, *de rigueur*. All good things must be taken in measure, however, and therefore it is critical that we let sanity and good taste prevail: as long as the first sip of the relevant caffeine- or hop-based beverage is taken while beads of sweat, snow or rain are still evident on one's brow, then it is legitimate for the cap to be worn. However, once all that remains in the cranial furrows is salt, it is then time to shower, throw on some suitable *après*-ride attire (a woollen Molteni Arcore training top *circa* '73 comes to mind) and return to the bar, folded copy of pastel-coloured news publication in hand, ready for formal fluid replacement. It is also helpful if you are a Giant of the Road, as demonstrated here, rather than a giant douchebag.

Rule #23 // Tuck only after reaching escape velocity.
You may only employ the aerodynamic tuck after you have spun out your 53 × 11; the tuck is to be engaged only when your legs can no longer keep up. Your legs make you go fast, and trying to keep your fat ass out of the wind only serves to keep you from slowing down once you reach escape velocity. Thus, the tuck is only to be employed to prevent you slowing down when your

legs have wrung the top end out of your block. Tucking prematurely while descending is the antithesis of Casually Deliberate. For more on riding fast downhill see Rule #64 and Rule #85.

Rule #24 // Speeds and distances shall be referred to and measured in kilometres.

This includes while discussing Cycling in the workplace with your non-cycling co-workers, serving to mystify our sport further in the web of their Neanderthalic cognitive capabilities. As the confused expression spreads across their unibrowed faces, casually mention your shaved legs. All of Cycling's Monuments are measured in the metric system, and therefore the English system is forbidden.

Rule #25 // The bikes on top of your car should be worth more than the car.

Or at least be relatively more expensive. Basically, if you're putting your Huffy on your Rolls, you're in trouble, mister. Remember what Sean said.

Rule #26 // Make your bike photogenic.

When photographing your bike, gussy her up properly for the camera. Some parameters are firm: valve stems at six o'clock. Cranks never at 90 or 180 degrees. Others are at your discretion, although the accepted practices include putting the chain on the big dog and no bidons in the cages.

Rule #27 // Shorts and socks should be like Goldilocks.

Not too long and not too short. (Disclaimer: despite Sean Yates's horrible choice in shorts length, he is a quintessential hardman of Cycling and is deeply admired by the Velominati. Whereas Armstrong's short and sock lengths are just plain wrong.) No socks is a no-no, as are those ankle-length ones which should only be worn by female tennis players.

Rule #28 // Socks can be any damn colour you like.
White is old-school cool. Black is cool too, but were given a bad image by a Texan whose socks were too long. If you feel you must go coloured, make sure they damn well match your kit. Tip: DeFeet Wooleators rule.

Rule #29 // No European posterior man-satchels.
Saddlebags have no place on a road bike, and are acceptable on mountain bikes only in extreme cases.

Rule #30 // No frame-mounted pumps.
Either CO_2 canisters or mini-pumps should be carried in jersey pockets (see Rule #31). The only exception to this rule is to mount a Silca brand frame pump in the rear triangle of the frame, with the rear wheel skewer as the pump mount knob, as demonstrated by members of the 7-Eleven and Ariostea Pro Cycling teams. As such, a frame pump mounted upside down and along the left (skewer lever side) seat stay is both old-school and Euro and thus acceptable. We restate at this time that said pump may under no circumstances be a Zefal and must be made by Silca. Said Silca pump must be fitted with a Campagnolo head. It is acceptable to gaffer-tape a mini-pump to your frame when no CO_2 canisters are available and your pockets are full of spare kit and energy gels. However, the rider should expect to be stopped and questioned and may be required to empty pockets to prove there is no room in them for the pump.

Rule #31 // Spare tubes, multi-tools and repair kits should be stored in jersey pockets.
Or, if absolutely necessary, in a converted bidon in a cage on the bike.

Rule #32 // Humps are for camels: no hydration packs.
Hydration packs are never to be seen on a road rider's body.

No argument will be entered into on this. For MTB, they are cool.

Rule #33 // Shave your guns.

Legs are to be carefully shaved at all times. If, for some reason, your legs are to be left hairy, make sure you can dish out plenty of hurt to shaved riders, or be considered a hippie douche on your way to a Critical Mass. Whether you use a straight razor or a Bowie knife, use Baxter to keep them smooth.

Rule #34 // Mountain bike shoes and pedals have their place.

On a mountain bike.

Rule #35 // No visors on the road.

Road helmets can be worn on mountain bikes, but never the other way around. If you want shade, see Rule #22.

Rule #36 // Eyewear shall be Cycling-specific.

No Aviator shades, blueblockers or clip-on covers for eyeglasses.

Rule #37 // The arms of the eyewear shall always be placed over the helmet straps.

No exceptions. This is for various reasons that may or may not matter; it's just the way it is.

Rule #38 // Don't play leapfrog.

Train properly: if you get passed by someone, it is nothing personal, just accept that on the day/effort/ride they were stronger than you. If you can't deal with it, work harder. But don't go playing leapfrog to get in front only to be overtaken again (multiple times) because you can't keep up the pace. Especially don't do this just because the person overtaking you is a woman. Seriously. Get over it.

Rule #39 // Never ride without your eyewear.
You should not make a habit of riding without eyewear, although approved extenuating circumstances include fog, overheating and lighting conditions. When not worn over the eyes, they should be neatly tucked into the vents of your helmet. If they don't fit, buy a new helmet. In the meantime you can wear them backwards on the back of your head or carefully tuck them into your jersey pocket, making sure not to scratch them on your tools (see Rule #31).

Rule #40 // Tyres are to be mounted with the label centred over the valve stem.
Pro mechanics do it because it makes it easier to find the valve. You do this because that's the way Pro mechanics do it. This will save you precious seconds while your fat ass sits on the roadside fumbling with your CO_2 after a puncture. It also looks better for photo opportunities. Note: this obviously applies only to clinchers as tubulars don't give you a choice.

Rule #41 // Quick-release levers are to be carefully positioned.
Quick-release angle on the front skewer shall be an upward angle which tightens just aft of the fork and the rear quick-release shall tighten at an angle that bisects the angle between the seat and chain stays. It is acceptable, however, to have the rear quick-release tighten upward, just aft of the seat stay, when the construction of the frame or its dropouts will not allow the preferred positioning. For time trial bikes only, quick releases may be in the horizontal position facing towards the rear of the bike. This is for maximum aero effect.

Rule #42 // A bike race shall never be preceded with a swim and/or followed by a run.
If it's preceded by a swim and/or followed by a run, it is not called a bike race, it is called a duathlon or a triathlon. Neither of which is

a bike race. Also keep in mind that one should only swim in order to prevent drowning, and should only run if being chased. And even then, one should only run fast enough to prevent capture.

Rule #43 // Don't be a jackass.
But if you absolutely must be a jackass, be a funny jackass. Always remember, we're all brothers and sisters on the road.

Rule #44 // Position matters.
In order to find the V-Locus, a rider's handlebars on their road bike must always be lower than their saddle. The only exception to this is if you're revolutionising the sport, in which case you must also be prepared to break the world Hour Record. The minimum allowable tolerance is 4 cm; there is no maximum, but people may berate you if they feel you have them too low.

Rule #45 // Slam your stem.
A maximum stack height of 2 cm is allowed below the stem and a single 5 mm spacer must always – always – be stacked above. A 'slammed-down' stack height is preferable, meaning that the stem is positioned directly on the top race of the headset.

Rule #46 // Keep your bars level.
Handlebars will be mounted parallel to the ground or angled slightly upward. While they may never be pointed down at all, they may be angled up slightly; allowed handlebar tilt is to be between 180 and 175 degrees with respect to the level road. The brake levers will preferably be mounted such that the end of the brake lever is even with the bottom of the bar. Modern bars, however, dictate that this may not always be possible, so tolerances are permitted within reason. Brake hoods should not approach anything near 45 degrees, as some riders with poor taste have been insisting on doing.

Rule #47 // Drink Tripels, don't ride triples.
Cycling and beer are so intertwined we may never understand the full relationship. Beer is a recovery drink, an elixir for post-ride trash talking and a just plain excellent thing to pour down the neck. We train to drink, so don't fool around. Drink quality beer from real breweries. If it is brewed with rice instead of malted barley or requires a lime, you are off the path. Know your bittering units like you know your gear length. Life is short; don't waste it on piss beer.

Rule #48 // Saddles must be level and pushed back.
The seating area of a saddle is to be visually level, with the base measurement made using a spirit level. Based on subtleties of saddle design and requirements of comfort, the saddle may then be pitched slightly forward or backward to reach a position that offers stability, power and comfort. If the tilt of the saddle exceeds 2 degrees, you need to go get one of those saddles with springs and a thick gel pad because you are obviously a big pussy. The midpoint of the saddle as measured from tip to tail shall fall well behind and may not be positioned forward of the line made by extending the seat tube through the top of the saddle. (Also see Rule #44.)

Rule #49 // Keep the rubber side down.
It is completely unacceptable to turn one's steed upside down deliberately for any reason under any circumstances. Besides the risk of scratching the saddle, levers and stem, it is unprofessional and a disgrace to your loyal steed. The risk of the bike falling over is increased, wheel removal/replacement is made more difficult and your bidons will leak. The only reason a bicycle should ever be in an upside-down position is during mid-rotation while crashing. This Rule also applies to upside down saddle-mount roof bars.

Rule #50 // Facial hair is to be carefully regulated.

No full beards, no moustaches. Goatees are permitted only if your name starts with 'Marco' and ends with 'Pantani', or if your head is intentionally or unintentionally bald. One may never shave on the morning of an important race as it saps your virility, and you need that to kick ass.

Rule #51 // Livestrong wristbands are cockrings for your arms.

While we hate cancer, isn't it better to just donate some money and not have to advertise the fact for the next five years? You may as well get 'tryhard wanker' tattooed on your forehead. Or you may well be a bogan.

Rule #52 // Drink in moderation.

Bidons are to be small in size: 500–610 ml maximum. No extra-large vessels are to be seen on one's machine. Two cages can be mounted, but only one bidon on rides under two hours is to be employed. Said solo bidon must be placed in the downtube cage only. You may only ride with a bidon in the rear cage if you have a front bidon, or you just handed your front bidon to a fan at the roadside and you are too busy crushing everyone to move it forward until you take your next drink. Bidons should match each other and preferably your bike and/or kit. The obvious exception is the classic Coca-Cola bidon, which by default matches any bike and/or kit owing to its heritage. Coca-Cola should only be consumed flat and near the end of a long ride or all-day solo breakaway on the roads of France.

Rule #53 // Keep your kit clean and new.

As a courtesy to those around you, your kit should always be freshly laundered, and under no circumstances should the crackal region of your shorts be worn out or see-through.

Rule #54 // No aerobars on road bikes.
Aerobars or other clip-on attachments are under no circumstances to be employed on your road bike. The only exception to
this is if you are competing in a mountain time trial.

Rule #55 // Earn your turns.
If you are riding down a mountain, you must first have ridden up
the mountain. It is forbidden to employ powered transportation
simply for the cheap thrill of descending. The only exception to
this is if you are doing intervals on L'Alpe d'Huez or the Plan
de Corones and you park your car up top before doing twenty
repeats of the climb.

Rule #56 // Espresso or macchiato only.
When wearing Cycling kit and enjoying a pre- or post-ride
coffee, it is only appropriate to drink espresso or macchiato.
If the word soy/skim latte is heard to be used by a member
wearing Cycling apparel, then that person must be ceremonially
beaten with CO_2 canisters or mini-pumps by others within the
community.

Rule #57 // No stickers.
Nobody gives a shit what causes you support, what war you're
against, what gear you buy or what year you rode RAGBRAI. See
Rule #5 and ride your bike. Decals, on the other hand, are not
only permissible but extremely Pro.

Rule #58 // Support your local bike shop.
Never buy bikes, parts or accessories online. Going into your
local shop, asking myriad inane questions, tying up the staff's
time and then going online to buy is akin to sleeping with your
best friend's wife, then having a beer with him after. If you do
purchase parts online, be prepared to mount and maintain them
yourself. If you enter a shop with parts you have bought online

and expect them to fit them, be prepared to be told to see your online seller for fitting and warranty help.

Rule #59 // Hold your line.
Ride predictably, and don't make sudden movements. And under no circumstances are you to deviate from your line.

Rule #60 // Ditch the washer-nut and valve-stem cap.
You are not, under any circumstances, to employ the use of the washer-nut and valve-stem cap that come with your inner tubes or tubulars. They are only supplied to meet shipping regulations. They are useless when it comes to tubes and tyres.

Rule #61 // Like your guns, saddles should be smooth and hard.
Under no circumstances may your saddle have more than 3 mm of padding. Special allowances will be made for stage racing when physical pain caused by subcutaneous cysts and the like ('saddle sores') are present. Under those conditions, up to 5 mm of padding will be allowed – it should be noted that this exception is only temporary until the condition has passed or been excised. A Hardman would not change their saddle at all but instead cut a hole in it to relieve pressure on the delicate area. It is noted that if Rule #48 and/or Rule #5 are observed, then any 'padding' is superfluous.

Rule #62 // You shall not ride with earphones.
Cycling is about getting outside and into the elements, and you don't need to be listening to Queen or Slayer in order to experience that. Immerse yourself in the rhythm and pain, not in whatever '80s hair band you call 'music'. See Rule #5 and ride your bike.

Rule #63 // Point in the direction you're turning.
Signal a left turn by pointing your left arm to the left. To signal a right turn, simply point with your right arm to the right. This one is, presumably, mostly for Americans: that right-turn signal that Americans are taught to make with your left arm elbow-out and your forearm pointing upwards was developed for motor vehicles prior to the invention of the electric turn signal, since it was rather difficult to reach from the driver-side all the way out the passenger-side window to signal a right turn. On a bicycle, however, we don't have this limitation, and it is actually quite easy to point your right arm in the direction you are turning. The American right-turn signal just makes you look like you're waving 'hello' to traffic.

Rule #64 // Cornering confidence increases with time and experience.
This pattern continues until it falls sharply and suddenly.

Rule #65 // Maintain and respect your machine.
Bicycles must adhere to the Principle of Silence and as such must be meticulously maintained. They must be cherished, and when leaned against a wall, they must be leaned carefully such that only the bars, saddle or tyres come in contact with the wall or post. This is true even when dismounting prior to collapsing after the World Championship Time Trial. No squeaks, creaks or chain noise allowed. Only the soothing hum of your tyres on the tarmac and the rhythm of your breathing may be audible when riding. When riding the *pavé*, the sound of chain slap is acceptable. The Principle of Silence can be extended to say that if you are suffering such that your breathing begins adversely to affect the enjoyment of the other riders in the bunch, you are to summarily sit up and allow yourself to be dropped.

Rule #66 // No mirrors.

Mirrors are allowed on your (aptly named) Surly Big Dummy or your Surly Long-Haul Trucker. Not on your road steed. Not on your mountain bike. Not on your helmet. If someone familiar with The Rules has sold you such an abomination, return the mirror and demand a refund, plus interest and damages.

Rule #67 // Do your time in the wind.

Nobody likes a wheel sucker. You might think you're playing a smart tactical game by letting everyone else do the work while you sit on, but races (even town sign sprints) are won through co-operation and spending time on the rivet, flogging yourself and taking risks. Riding wheels and jumping past at the end is one thing and one thing only: poor sportsmanship.

Rule #68 // Rides are to be measured by quality, not quantity.

Rides are to be measured by the quality of their distance and never by distance alone. For climbing rides, distances should be referred to by the amount of vertical covered; flat and rolling rides should be referred to by their distance and average speed. For example, declaring 'We rode 4 km' would assert that 4,000 metres were climbed during the ride, with the distance being irrelevant. Conversely, a flat ride of 150 km at 23 kph is not something that should be discussed in an open forum, and Rule #5 must be reviewed at once.

Rule #69 // Cycling shoes and bicycles are made for riding.

Any walking conducted while wearing Cycling shoes must be strictly limited. When taking a slash or filling bidons during a 200 km ride (at 38 kph, see Rule #68) one is to stow one's bicycle carefully at the nearest point navigable by bike and walk the remaining distance. It is strictly prohibited under any circumstances for a Cyclist to walk up a steep incline, the obvious exception being when said incline is blocked by riders who crashed because you are on the Koppenberg. For clarification, see Rule #5.

Rule #70 // The purpose of competing is to win.
End of. Any reference to not achieving this should be referred immediately to Rule #5.

Rule #71 // Train properly.
Know how to train properly and stick to your training plan. Ignore other Cyclists with whom you are not intentionally riding. The time for being competitive is not during your training rides but during competition.

Rule #72 // Legs speak louder than words.
Unless you routinely demonstrate your riding superiority and the smoothness of your stroke, refrain from discussing your power meter, heart rate or any other riding data. Also see Rule #74.

Rule #73 // Gear and brake cables should be cut to optimum length.
Cables should create a perfect arc around the headtube and, whenever possible, cross under the downtube. Right shifter cable should go to the left cable stop and vice versa.

Rule #74 // V-Meters or small computers only.
Forgo the data and ride on feel: little compares to the pleasure of riding as hard as your mind will allow. Learn to read your body, meditate on Rule #5 and learn to push yourself to your limit. Power meters, heart rate monitors and GPS are bulky, ugly and superfluous. Any cycle computer, if deemed necessary, should be simple, small, mounted on the stem and wireless.

Rule #75 // Race numbers are for races.
Remove it from your frame before the next training ride because, no matter how cool you think it looks, it does not look cool. Unless you are in a race. In which case it looks cool.

Rule #76 // Helmets are to be hung from your stem.
When not worn, helmets are to be clipped to the stem and draped over your handlebars.

Rule #77 // Respect the earth: don't litter.
Cycling is not an excuse to litter. Do not throw your empty gel packets, energy bar wrappers or punctured tubes on the road or in the bush. Stuff them in your jersey pockets and repair that tube when you get home.

Rule #78 // Remove unnecessary gear.
When racing in a criterium of 60 minutes or less, the second (unused) water bottle cage must be removed in order to preserve the aesthetic of the racing machine.

Rule #79 // Fight for your town lines.
Town lines must be contested or at least faked if you're not into it or too shagged to do anything but pedal the bike.

Rule #80 // Always be casually deliberate.
Waiting for others pre-ride or at the start line pre-race, you must be *tranquilo*, resting on your top tube. This may be extended to any time one is aboard the bike, but not riding it, such as at stop lights.

Rule #81 // Don't talk it up.
Rides and crashes may only be discussed and recounted in detail when the rider required external assistance in recovery or recuperation. Otherwise refer to Rule #5.

Rule #82 // Close the gap.
While riding in cold and/or Rule #9 conditions replete with arm warmers, under no circumstances is there to be any exposed skin between the hems of your kit and the hems of your arm warmers. If this occurs, you either need to wear a kit that fits you properly or increase the size of your guns. Arm warmers may, however, be shoved to the wrists in Five And Dime scenarios, particularly those involving Rule #9 conditions. The No-Gap Principle also applies to knee and leg warmers, with the variation that these are under no circumstances to be scrunched down around the ankles; Merckx have mercy on whoever is caught in such a sad, sorry state. It is important to note that while one can wear arm warmers without wearing knee or leg warmers, one cannot wear knee or leg warmers without wearing arm warmers (or a long-sleeve jersey). It is completely inappropriate to have uncovered arms while covering the knees, with the exception of brief periods of time when the arm warmers may be shoved to the wrists while going uphill in a Five And Dime situation. If the weather changes and one must remove a layer, the knee/leg coverings must go before the arm coverings. If that means that said rider must take off his knee or leg warmers while racing, then this is a skill he must be accomplished in. The single exception would be before an event in which someone plans on wearing neither arm or leg warmers while racing, but would like to keep the legs warm before the event starts; though wearing a long sleeve jersey over the racing kit at this time is also advised. One must not forget to remove said leg warmers.

Rule #83 // Be self-sufficient.
Unless you are followed by a team car, you will repair your own punctures. You will do so expediently, employing your own skills, using your own equipment and without complaining that your expensive tyres are too tight for your puny thumbs to fit over your expensive rim. The fate of a rider who has failed to

equip himself pursuant to Rule #31, or who knows not how to use said equipment, shall be determined at the discretion of any accompanying or approaching rider in accordance with Rule #84.

Rule #84 // Follow the Code.
Consistently with The Code of the *Domestique*, the announcement of a flat tyre in a training ride entitles – but does not oblige – all riders then present in the bunch to cease riding without fear of being labelled Pussies. All stopped riders are thereupon entitled – but not obliged – to lend assistance, instruction and/or stringent criticism of the tyre mender's technique. The duration of a Rule #84 stop is entirely discretionary, but is generally inversely proportional to the duration of the remaining time available for post-ride espresso.

Rule #85 // Descend like a Pro.
All descents shall be undertaken at speeds commonly regarded as 'ludicrous' or 'insane' by those less talented. In addition all corners will be traversed in an outside-inside-outside trajectory, with the outer leg extended and the inner leg canted appropriately (but not too far as to replicate a motorcycle racer, for you are not one), to assist in balance and creation of an appealing aesthetic. Brakes are generally not to be employed, but if absolutely necessary, only just prior to the corner. Also see Rule #64.

Rule #86 // Don't half-wheel.
Never half-wheel your riding partners; it's terrible form – it is always the other guy who sets the pace. Unless, of course, you are on the rivet, in which case it's an excellent intimidation technique.

Rule #87 // The ride starts on time. No exceptions.
The upside of always leaving on time is considerable. Others will be late exactly once. You signal that the sanctity of this ride,

like all rides, is not something with which you should muck about. You demonstrate, not with words but with actions, your commitment. As a bonus, you make more time for post-ride espresso. 'On Time', of course, is taken to mean at V past the hour or half-hour.

Rule #88 // Don't surge.

When rolling on to the front to take your turn in the wind, see Rule #67: do not suddenly lift the pace unless trying to establish a break. The key to maintaining a high average speed is to work with your companions and allow no gaps to form in the line. It is permissible to lift the pace gradually, and if this results in people being dropped, then they have been ridden off your wheel and are of no use to the bunch anyway. If you are behind someone who jumps on the pedals when they hit the front, do not reprimand the offender with cries of 'Don't Surge' unless the offender is a Frenchman named Serge.

Rule #89 // Pronounce it correctly.

All races shall be referred to by the name given in their country of origin, and care shall be taken to pronounce the name as well as possible. For Belgian races it is preferable to choose the name given in its region of origin, though the use of either the Flemish or Wallonian pronunciation is at the speaker's discretion. This principle shall also be extended to apply to riders' names, bicycle and component marques and Cycling accoutrements.

Rule #90 // Never get out of the big ring.

If it gets steeper, just push harder on the pedals. When pressed on the matter, the Apostle Johan Museeuw simply replied, 'Yes, why would you slow down?' It is, of course, acceptable momentarily to shift into the inner ring when scaling the 20 per cent ramps of the Kapelmuur.

Rule #91 // No food on training rides under four hours.
This one also comes from the Apostle Johan Museeuw, who said to Frank: 'Yes, no food on rides under four hours. You need to lose some weight.' Or, as Fignon put it, sometimes, when we train, we simply have to go out to meet The Man with the Hammer. The exception is, of course, hard rides over two hours and races. Also, if you're planning on being out for more than four hours, start eating before you get hungry. This also applies to energy drink supplements.

Rule #92 // No sprinting from the hoods.
The only exception is riders whose name starts with Giuseppe and ends with Saronni. See the Goodwood Worlds in '82.

Rule #93 // Descents are not for recovery; recovery ales are for recovery.
Descents are meant to be as hard and demanding as – and much more dangerous than – the climbs. Climb hard, descend to close a gap or open one. Descents should hurt, not be a time for recovery. Recovery is designated only for the pub and for shit-talking.

Rule #94 // Use the correct tool for the job, and use the tool correctly.
Bicycle maintenance is an art; tools are designed to serve specific purposes, and it is essential that the Velominatus learns to use each tool properly when working on their loyal machine.

Rule #95 // Never lift your bike over your head.
Under no circumstances is it acceptable to raise one's machine above one's head. The only exception is when placing it on to a car's roof rack.

FURTHER READING

If you've already read *The Rules*, and now *The Hardmen*, you have exhausted the published works by Velominati. Having narrowly survived that experience, you must be ready to read some proper books on Cycling: ones that inspired us to write our own. For a more comprehensive list of recommended titles, visit The Works on Velominati at http://www.velominati.com/the-works/.

Rouleur magazine

Strictly a periodical rather than a book, *Rouleur* is immaculately curated and written. The entire project is founded on everything that makes the Velominati what we are: unbridled passion coupled to attention to detail bordering on the obsessive. Every issue drips with the culture, history and aesthetics of Cycling, conveyed through articles by legends such as Robert Millar, in-depth and fully geeky interviews, such as with Chris Boardman on the selection of Royce hubs for his Hour Record attempt, and a detailed series on, for example, how to select and mount tubular tyres properly.

Need for the Bike // Paul Fournel

While one would have to go a long way to find a book whose cover is less Rule-compliant, inside, *Need for the Bike* (also published in illustrated form as *Vélo)* is an absolute masterpiece of imagery. It comprises a series of short passages on discrete topics that encapsulate what life aboard two wheels means to each of us, all written in the most beautiful prose. If *Rouleur* is the Velominati's inspiration in structure, then *Need for the Bike* was our inspiration in style.

Tomorrow, We Ride // Jean Bobet
Perhaps the single most inspirational work on what it means to love the bicycle. Jean Bobet takes us on a journey through his life as a scholar and professional Cyclist alongside his famous brother Louison, who won the Tour de France three times. In some places historical, in others touching, in others it is downright funny. But mostly, it's about a love of life as a Cyclist.

Le Métier // Michael Barry
Le Métier (meaning 'the craft' or 'the work') is always *just* this side of addiction in Michael Barry's beautifully written account of the struggle of professional Cycling, an existence redeemed by the beauty of life above a top tube. He immaculately describes the shifting nature of racing and training as it changes with the seasons.

The Rider // Tim Krabbe
'To say that the race is the metaphor for life is to miss the point. The race is everything. It obliterates whatever isn't racing. Life is the metaphor for the race.' If *Tomorrow, We Ride* is the most inspirational work on what it means to love the bicycle, then *The Rider* is the most comprehensive description of what it means to be a racer. Translated masterfully from Dutch into English, Krabbe's masterpiece intimately captures the essence of the road racer, his hardship, pain and joy, all laid bare on the roads of a single day's racing in the Tour du Mont Aigoual.

ACKNOWLEDGEMENTS

Since writing our first book, *The Rules*, very little has changed in the approach that the Velominati have taken to sharing in our passion for Cycling. We still love the bike, the sport and the singular beauty that can be found in a life on two wheels. We prefer to discuss Cycling over any other subject, and the community on Velominati.com continues to be our major source of inspiration, sense of community and pride.

It is the spirit of openness, of sharing and communication of the community at Velominati that has brought us to the point where we have the opportunity to bore you with a second book. Each and every community member has contributed to making Velominati a unique entity in the world of Cycling. Their boundless love of all things Cycling and their unbridled need and desire to argue tubular tyres versus clinchers for days and days is commendable. These are our people; this is the shaved-legged tribe we will defend and ride with for ever. From the bottom of our hearts we still thank you each and every one.

We would like to thank a few people who have been particularly helpful and inspiring. First is James Spackman, our fearless agent, long-suffering editor on *Hardmen* and dear friend. He should rightly be listed as an author for the amount of rewriting required of him, but having this book on his CV could only be a liability. He negotiated multiple new deadlines for us to ignore. With his directional input and editing he has really earned what he will probably not be compensated for. Many a night he must have bitterly complained to his family over dinner and worried whether this book would ever take shape.

Then there is Frank's family – Andrine, Otto, Erik and Karen – who all helped him discover and cultivate a love for the bike at a young age, riding together on sacred roads all over Europe. Also Gianni, whose friendship and incorruptible sense of humour together with an undying willingness to continue pushing to the finish was a major force behind this book's completion. Gianni would like to thank his wife and Cycling partner, Beth, for putting up with his Cycling obsession (but she was warned – he was like that when she met him). He would also like to thank his other riding friends who still let him join a Sunday ride. It is appreciated more than they know.

Brett would like to thank the deadline gods who somehow always leave it to the last minute to reveal their magic date, and then take mercy on him by being perpetually non-punctual themselves. And Gianni, for being the constant force behind getting this thing done, James for his patience and Frank for the new swear words. And his dad, for finding him classic bikes in piles of junk, and mum, for letting him fill the shed with them.

PICTURE CREDITS

HARDMAN BIOGRAPHIES

(Written by their fellow Keepers, to maintain 'integrity')

Frank Strack // The founder of Velominati, Frank was born in the Dutch colonies of Minnesota. His boundless physical talents are carefully cancelled out by his equally boundless enthusiasm for drinking. Coffee, beer, wine: if it's in a container, he will enjoy it – a lot of it. He currently lives in Seattle. He loves riding in the rain and scheduling visits with The Man with the Hammer, just to be reminded of the privilege it is to feel completely depleted. He holds down a technology job the description of which no one really understands, and his interests outside Cycling and drinking are Cycling and drinking.

Everyone who sees his bike can't imagine what human could ride it. That seat is too high, those bars too low; well, Frank looks prefect on it. He is the Dutch Monkey, after all: he makes it his business to look the business on the bike.

John 'Gianni' Andrews // Much less Italian than Frank is Dutch, John grew up in Massachusetts but emigrated to Hawaii for the year-round Cycling and to escape from the smouldering wreck that was his science career. He has the athletic capacities of a pre-teen asthmatic with premature male-pattern baldness.

When the French pathologist opens him for his autopsy, the pathologist will be heard to mutter, '*C'est vrai? Un Cycliste? Wiz a heart zee size of a citron? C'est impossible.*' Laconic, dry and infuriatingly sharp, Gianni can turn any mediocre occasion into a hedonistic knees-up with a deftly timed quip without breaking stride or any furniture.

Brett Kennedy // A self-loathing Australian now living in Wellington, New Zealand, he fancies himself more Kiwi than Aussie. His passions include holding grudges and smoking cigarettes before crushing fools off the front on the cobblestones of northern Europe. He comes to road Cycling by way of mountain bikes, hence his clueless defence of non-white Cycling socks. Beyond Velominati he curates the Cycling lifestyle website ChainslapMag.com and keeps his fingers on the pulse of the Cycling industry by working part-time in a bike shop (also because it is the only of his endeavours that pays a living wage). He rides road, mountain and gravel bikes and is maddeningly good at riding on the front despite being out all night as the scourge of Lille's nightlife.